MW00934908

Agony and Absurdity: Adventures in Cancerland

Young Women and Breast Cancer

An Anthology

Edited by Meaghan Calcari Campbell,
Laurie Hessen Pomeranz and
Robin Bruns Worona

Copyright © 2016 Bay Area Young Survivors (BAYS)

All rights reserved.

Cover image © Maxiphoto

ISBN: 978-1537095455

"When you are in the middle of a story it isn't a story at all, but only a confusion; a dark roaring, a blindness, a wreckage of shattered glass and splintered wood; like a house in a whirlwind, or else a boat crushed by the icebergs or swept over the rapids, and all aboard powerless to stop it. It's only afterwards that it becomes anything like a story at all. When you are telling it, to yourself or to someone else."

— Margaret Atwood, *Alias Grace*

Contents

IV.   RELATIONSHIPS

V.   ILLUMINATION

VI.   NEW NORMAL?

VII.   ABSURDITIES

Introduction

Meaghan Calcari Campbell,
Laurie Hessen Pomeranz and
Robin Bruns Worona

There is nothing like the smell of San Francisco's Mission District on a Saturday night, right at the intersection of Mission and 18th Streets. Bacon-wrapped hotdogs. Beer. Exhaust. Weed. And the ever-present tinge of Ocean. Mostly those hotdogs, though.

That's where our minds were the night we realized we had more stories to tell. The Bay Area Young Survivors (BAYS), a support group for women diagnosed with breast cancer before the age of forty-five, had just wrapped-up an evening of storytelling at San Francisco's 2015 Litquake, an annual literary festival with readings in spots all across the Mission District, from laundry mats to sex clubs, bars to taquerias.

On the walk home, Laurie and Meaghan were laughing, recalling the imagery in Robin's newest tale about being at a "healing event" that involved batting balloons around the room with elderly women in pastel—and *only* pastel—clothing.

And then, we remembered an email exchange on the BAYS listserve from earlier that day. One of our members had posted that her friend's mom was in town and had forgotten her breast prosthesis. She was a C-cup, did anyone have a spare breast they could lend her for the week? Laurie wrote back quickly, before heading out the door to work, "I left a boob on my doorstep for you."

High on joy and those bacon-wrapped-hotdog fumes, Laurie said, "We have to do a next book, and we have to focus on the absurdities of all of this."

The next day, we floated the idea to the over four hundred BAYS members. The response was just as we had hoped—enthusiastic and affirmative. We realized that while many of us have some distance and are able to laugh again, there are many other women just starting with us, in the thick of it, getting through the diagnosis days. And, there are women, far too many, who have died from this disease—absurd, yes, but funny, no. The book would need to address the range of experiences.

The wonderful thing about BAYS is that we are like a living, breathing, growing organism. We live, we die. We laugh, we weep. Sometimes we laugh because it's so ludicrous, sometimes we laugh to keep from crying, and sometimes we just wail. And, sometimes we wail until we start laughing. We do it together. Finding ourselves in a strange new world, a topsy turvy place, this Cancerland, where the ground seems to shift without warning beneath our feet, we try our best to hold on to each other. To provide a bit of sanity and stability for our sisters. Some shelter from the cancer storm.

So, one year after that fragrant night in the Mission, we present our third collection of personal narratives, once more honoring the memory of our late BAYS sister Erin Williams Hyman, who first conceived of a BAYS anthology. She brought us the book *The Day My Nipple Fell Off*, and inspired the second book *Shivering in a Paper Gown*. Forty-one authors stepped forward from BAYS to put their experiences and recollections into words here. And, while these stories may be from a moment in time, in many ways, they are timeless.

In these pages, we take a look at both the public and private faces of breast cancer. The agony and the absurdity. We look behind the curtain, underneath the paper gown, to see our ever-changing bodies and perspectives, and the ongoing search for a semblance of "new normal," which occurs at each phase of the breast cancer experience. The adjustments to our bodies, our diagnoses, our remissions and recurrences and metastases, and our sense of the future, are ongoing.

We are young, launching our lives and careers, our relationships and families. Then, cancer plops down in the middle of it all. We are forced to face the most important decisions of our lives without any forewarning. Freezing embryos? I wasn't even sure I wanted kids, and oh, I can't afford to harvest anyway. Taking a year off work? But, I'm a feminist on the cusp of a world-altering career. Always wanted to be a mom and breastfeed?

Fuck this. Cancer is robbing me of my fertility and my breasts at the same damn time.

You may cringe at some of the thoughtless things people say to us. You may weep at the suffering and the loss that are revealed in these stories. At the same time, you will see the power, authenticity and humor embodied by this group of fierce women.

We write because it helps us to heal. It helps us to process what the hell is happening to us. It helps us to connect with ourselves, and to step out of the isolation of the cancer experience and shine a light that helps us to look inside, where it can be dark, scary and hard to see.

In offering you these stories, we give you a piece of our lives that has shaped us in profound ways, both painful and powerful. We welcome you in, and trust that in recording these tales, we move our healing forward, remembering where we've been, how far we've come, and how we want to live in this present moment. We hope to increase understanding of the young patient and survivor experience, and to illuminate the dark spaces for those who will walk this path in the future.

This is our gift to ourselves and each other, and to you.

Thank you for joining us.

I. IN THE BEGINNING

"Severe illness wasn't life-altering, it was life-shattering. It felt less like an epiphany—a piercing burst of light, illuminating What Really Matters—and more like someone had just firebombed the path forward."

— Paul Kalanithi, *When Breath Becomes Air*

"Life changes fast.
Life changes in the instant.
You sit down to dinner and life as you know it ends."

— Joan Didion, *The Year of Magical Thinking*

Tick Tick Tick Tick

Lindsay Jean Thomson

I can't tell if she's concerned or just concentrating. I don't want to believe that there's anything to be concerned about, so I decide she must just have one of those deep-thinking faces. "Well, it doesn't look like a cyst..." she says.

It doesn't look like a cyst because it isn't a cyst.

Monday

Four days later, I'm back for a mammogram and ultrasound.

The mammogram technician is a third generation San Franciscan. She tries to distract me with small talk and I let her. "What do you do? Where are you from?"

My turn. "How long have you been doing this?"

"Thirty-seven years."

Longer than I've been alive.

It seems like she's taking a lot of x-rays. I lose count. This feels like a bad sign.

"Are you crying because I'm hurting you?"

No.

It does hurt though. Because I'm young and my breast tissue is dense, they have to apply a lot of pressure in order to get a good image. I can see the x-rays on the screen and they're kind of beautiful in a strange way; the orb of my breast lit up with this newly discovered supernova. Otherworldly. My very own exploding star. *How could something so pretty be so bad?*

Luckily I'm not shy about being naked. Getting a mammogram is like the world's least sexy photo shoot. "Turn a little to the left. A little bit more. Lift your chin. Hold your breath. Don't move don't move don't move!"

She leaves to show the doctor what she's found and then returns to take more images.

By the time she takes me to the ultrasound, she can't even make eye contact with me anymore. I don't blame her. I imagine that this many years of breaking bad news would wear on a person.

I've spent virtually no time in a waiting room today, though it all feels like waiting. I watch the seconds of the clock because it's easier than watching the disappointment on the sonographer's face. When I can't stand looking at the *tick tick tick tick*, my eyes wander to the ceiling. I study every seam, every symmetry, every irregularity. There's a long, narrow piece missing near the cupboards, and I can't decide which bothers me more: that it's not there or that I can't remember what it's called. What the fuck is that called? Particle board? It's not particle board. I still don't know.

I've been here for more than two hours and start to wonder if

I've gotten a parking ticket yet. I mean, *come on.*

The doctor arrives and they speak some foreign language. He's curt with the ultrasound technician; she's never standing in just the right place. She doesn't anticipate what he needs before he needs it. I don't like it.

Tick tick tick tick.

This clock is all tick and no tock. What's *that* about?

"What's the likelihood that someone my age with no family history of breast cancer—of any kind cancer—would get it?"

"It's not common but it's not rare."

Ok.

When he finishes the exam, he removes his gloves with an efficient snap and washes his hands briskly. Doctorly.

"I'm *very* concerned," he says. "This is *worrisome.*" He doesn't fucking look concerned. In addition to the main lump that I can feel, they've found at least two more—including one in my lymph nodes. Large portions of my breast are calcified. "It looks like cancer. And when it looks like cancer, it's usually cancer…"

This is deeply offensive to me. *Yo, doctor. Imma let you finish, but I have some of the best breasts of all time. The best breasts of all time!*

I cry, and he says nothing to make me feel better.

They tell me it's time for their lunch break and I can come back in half an hour for the biopsy. When I leave, I burst into tears again and call my best friend. She doesn't answer, but I know that she knows where I am today, and I know that the simple act of my calling in the middle of the day will worry her.

My car doesn't have a parking ticket—a minor miracle. I'll take it.

The biopsy isn't that bad. The worst part is keeping my arm over head, which causes it to both go numb and cramp at the same time. I make a lame joke about it, and, for the first time, the doctor cracks a smile.

"Your new favorite position!" he says. *Did he just make a sex joke?* Maybe I like him a little bit after all.

They do three biopsies: one of the large mass that brought me in, one in my armpit, and one closer to my nipple. Each time he walks me through the process as if I haven't heard him say it before.

"Now I'm going to clean the area. Now I'm going to numb it. Now you'll feel a cold gel. Now I'll numb a little deeper." The machine sounds like a staple gun. He counts, "one, two, three," but he never does it at three, which makes me wonder why he bothers counting at all. I make the mistake of looking. I only feel one of them, and he gives me more lidocaine to numb it.

He leaves. "How long have you been doing this?" I ask the technician. "Eleven years." "And him?" "He's the chief," she says. *Oh.*

"Do you have Tylenol at home?"

"No, why? Am I going to be in pain?"

"Well, yeah. You had three biopsies."

Ok.

They tell me they'll call as soon as they get the results back. Not to shower for a day and not to lift or move anything for two or three. That I should bring someone with me next time.

Ok.

After the biopsies, I have to get more x-rays. This time I have a different technician, and I'm glad, because I don't know that I can handle seeing my old friend the third generation San Franciscan again.

Exactly three and a half hours, four band-aids, $134, and— *likely*—a cancer diagnosis later, I get to go.

I'm supposed to go to a bachelorette party this weekend. I debate about whether or not to tell the bride. Her mom died of cancer. A wedding is not just a celebration but also a sharp reminder of someone who is supposed to be there but isn't.

I decide that in the event I can't go, it would be better for her to have a few days to process it than to spring it on her right before it's time to party. She can't stop saying "fuck." After a few minutes, she starts to cry and tells me she has to go and will call me later.

It's ok, I'd cry too.

I start making a mental list of all of the people I'm going to have to call, but I don't know how many more of these I can do.

Paula and Kim come over for dinner. Paula brings cake and

Kim a nice bottle of rosé and a roasted chicken. And flowers. I admire this in a friend: the ability to turn anything into a celebration.

Mostly, it's like any other night. I can tell they've talked though. Brave faces never look that brave. I tell them how anxious I am about having to call so many people—I don't know why this is my biggest concern, but it is. Paula suggests a phone tree. This seems like cruel and unusual punishment to inflict upon my loved ones.

Tuesday

I wake up sore and surprised, glad for the Tylenol. Mostly, I feel fine. I definitely don't feel sick. Occasionally, I burst into tears. I buy food I don't want to eat. Mostly, I'm waiting.

Tick tick tick tick. A ticking fucking time bomb.

I go to work because what else can I do? I make plans that I might not want to keep. I skip dinner.

Wednesday

I'm even more sore, but maybe it's just in my mind. I need to do laundry, but I'm pretty sure I'm not supposed to lift anything still.

Lis and I have brunch. She brings flowers, too. The phone rings. I think it's my doctor, but it's just a delivery guy.

I go to meetings. We host an event. Someone I barely know

says, "Hey, so-and-so told me…I just want you to know…"

Thoughts and prayers. Thoughts and prayers.

Thursday

One of my bruises is getting larger, and I use it as pretext to call. I get passed around a few times. My results are in, but they're not sure who is supposed to give them to me. The chief radiologist is out for the day.

The doorbell rings. More flowers.

The doctor calls. *Finally.* All three biopsies confirm that I have breast cancer. It's Grade III—this refers to how abnormal the cells are. What's the stage, or how far it has spread? He doesn't have a clear answer for me; at the very least, it has spread to my lymph nodes.

I can't tell you how many times someone asks "How are you?" in casual conversation in a week.

Ok.

Two weeks ago, I wrote about an essay about how to find meaningful work. I ended with this: "Most importantly, decide that you're going to be ok no matter what, and you will be."

Trying to be ok.

Chapter 1: The "C" Word

Maya

"It is cancer."

It was November 10th when I heard those dreaded words.

I was in a doctor's office in Santa Clara, California. A sterile room with white lights, a couple of uncomfortable chairs, a computer and an examination table. Neil was in a corner chair wearing his hoodie. The hoodie that I so disliked. To me, it was a constant reminder of the San Francisco urban-hipster-brogrammer culture—that I felt was contrived, pretentious and perhaps even a little sexist. Even though both of us are techies, we lived on opposite ends of the Silicon Valley High-Tech world. Neil had San Francisco as his base and blended in with the youth and energy of the city. I worked in an established corporation in the South Bay—the mature Silicon Valley.

We had been joking about work, as the doctor's assistant led us into the room. Being together at 5pm on a Thursday was a rare luxury, and we were making the most of it, largely ignoring the reason we were there: the pain in my breast that had been going on for a few months, the biopsy results just in. Then, the doctor walked in, her face somber.

17

I had been in this office five months earlier. She had looked at me like every other time, with a glance that said, "You're paranoid." But, she went ahead and ordered a mammogram and an ultrasound. This was the second time in a couple of years I had those tests. And like the last time, after reviewing the report, she said, "You have very dense breasts, but everything looks fine. Monitor if these lumps change with your cycle and come back in a few months if it's still an issue."

In October, right before I headed to Grace Hopper Celebration for Women in Computing, I felt a hardness right below the nipple. And the pain was getting hard to ignore. Of course, I wanted to forget about it and have fun at the conference with twelve thousand driven and talented women in computing gathered under one roof. The conference has been gaining momentum in recent years and has become increasingly star-studded with the Sheryl Sandbergs and the Megan Smiths of the world in attendance. No hoodies there!

I heard inspiring talks, had engaging conversations and came back highly energized. Immediately following the conference, my family visited. With family at home and Durga Puja, the lavish Autumn Festival characteristic of the part of the world I am from, every day was packed with activities, social gatherings, colorful sarees and mouth-watering food that put my healthy-eating plans on hold. But, my worry was not lost in all of the mayhem. I finally made the doctor's appointment and knew that I would ask for a biopsy no matter what.

The biopsy was scheduled for November 4th, the day before my fortieth birthday.

On November 3rd, my closest friends took me out for a birthday dinner. The three of us spent the evening in a Palo Alto watering hole, surrounded by the surreal Silicon Valley successes. We talked like we always do—about life and love, careers and passions, travel and adventure. There was a toast made to good health, too. It prompted me to tell them about the impending biopsy, yet in a very dismissive way. Sure, I was having a biopsy, but it would likely come back benign. My little sister had the same thing happen to her about a decade back. It would be the same for me! Sure, my paternal cousin had breast cancer at age twenty-nine. But, because her mother also had it, I was certain that the increased risk, if any, was part of a different genetic pool. I was convinced of being as much at risk as the girl next door. In fact, I was so blindly unconcerned, that I also sent my boss a very aggressive career plan that same day, off the heels of the inspiring tech conference.

On November 4th, like every other work-day morning, I drove down the scenic highway 280 South to work, with just a small detour in Mountain View for the biopsy. Needles, compression, bandages, then on my way to my desk at work.

And, to celebrate my birthday, I partied late into the night and throughout the whole weekend, conveniently forgetting the biopsy.

Then, it was November 10th. My doctor's office called,

requesting that I come in to get the results. I had planned to meet a cousin for dinner that night. I cancelled. This was our annual birthday ritual, but it had to wait. Neil decided to leave work early and come with me. While we drove to the doctor's office, we discussed what the worst case scenario could be. He was convinced that if we were ready for the worst case, aka cancer, then nothing we heard would be upsetting. Oh, the naiveté!

That brings us back to those three words.

It was like they weren't directed at me. We must have been talking about some random biopsy sample, another human being, a mix-up. It definitely wasn't me.

Neil burst into tears. The only thing I could think about was what was going to happen to this guy who I have built a life with and love so dearly.

Just three words that would change our lives forever.

Siri, I Have Cancer

Andrea Ghoorah Sieminski

It's 10am on a Wednesday, and I just received a call at work telling me that I have breast cancer. I go numb.

I immediately leave work and call my husband Paul from the car. I start crying hysterically. I can tell he's reeling too. He maintains his composure and comforts me but tries to quickly get us off the phone. I suspect he needs to pace around, clench his fists, and, possibly, scream out loud. He needs to process this in his own way. I let him off the hook and tell him I'll call my friend Ami.

Ami is a breast cancer survivor and one of the most honest, direct people I know. She'll shoot straight with me. I had called her the prior day to tell her that I'd gone in for a mammogram, ultrasound and biopsy. We both knew that this situation was not unfolding well. Most people who go in for a mammogram and ultrasound can walk out the door after the tech gets the pictures. Not me. I was left lying on the table and told to wait while the radiologist reviewed my film. The radiologist came into the room, repeated the ultrasound and told me that he'd like to do a biopsy, right then and there. There was a sense of urgency in his tone and manner, so I quickly consented. Within two minutes, I was prepped with iodine and sterile towels. It all happened so fast, I barely had time to get a text off to Paul telling him that they were doing a biopsy. When I told Ami how these events unfolded, her cancer radar went up, but she played it off so that I wouldn't worry. I know my friend well, though. I can tell when she's biting her tongue.

Flash forward twenty-four hours to when I call Ami from the car and get her voicemail. Next thing I know, I get a text from her, "I'm on the subway, let me call you in ten." Since I was driving, I use Siri on my iPhone to text back, "I have cancer." My phone rang a second later. Poor Ami is on BART, the Bay Area subway, and our conversation is fair game for all to hear. She's no longer playing anything off. The fact that they biopsied so quickly, my results came back in under twenty-four hours, AND they wanted me to meet the nurse coordinator the same day as my results was a trifecta she couldn't withhold comment on. I tell her that I had zoned out when the doctor called to deliver the cancer news (We've all watched enough TV to know this is a perfectly normal reaction!). I tell her that I recall hearing the words "aggressive," "ductal," and "infiltrating." Ami asks if I want the truth or if I want sugar-coating. I want the truth.

I go numb for the second time that day.

The Face

Kate Holcombe

Face *n.* **1.** the front of the head from the top of the forehead to the bottom of the chin, and from ear to ear; visage, countenance **2.** The expression of the countenance **3.** In cancer-speak, an expression of the countenance upon hearing of another's cancer diagnosis, generally of pained, forced and/or false empathy or pity, aimed at the diagnosed, and often but not always used to mask one's own inner terror at the news.

My first experience of "the face" occurred the day after my doctor called with the news that the lump I had found in the shower on Mother's Day, just a few days earlier, was breast cancer. She asked me to report to the cancer center the next day at 8:30am. While I have experienced many versions of "the face" since then, this began my introduction to this seemingly universal phenomenon.

My husband and our young daughter accompanied me to the appointment that morning—we had erroneously imagined it would only be a couple of hours, so a toddler in tow made sense. Over the next nine hours of exams, biopsies, scans, procedures, and consultations, we had many opportunities to experience several different versions of "the face," though they all went something like this:

A nurse, tech, doctor, radiologist, genetic counselor, or specialist (I saw them all!) comes in the room asking, "How are you today, Ms. Holcombe?" intent with some information, request or instruction they wish to share with me, and usually holding a clipboard or paper of some sort.

"Oh, fine, you know, aside from a few aberrant cells," I say, smiling.

Then they notice my daughter, with her bright and charming grin, happily greeting them.

"Is that your daughter?" they ask, starting to look sick.

"Why, yes," either my husband or I answer.

"Oh…" The wincing starts. "How old is she?" They can barely get the words out and have forgotten completely about the paper or clipboard they are holding and whatever news or task for me they had.

"She just turned one," we say.

"Oh…uh… wow," they manage to spit out, as their face crumples, their color draining, truly looking like they are about to vomit, sometimes even clutching their stomach. They might manage a quick "She's really cute," or "How adorable," before bolting from the room.

I turn to my husband and ask, "Do you think they are actually throwing up when they leave the room like that? Or just standing outside the door trying to collect themselves? Generally, not a good sign when the hospital staff can't even keep their shit together, is it?"

They'd usually come back a minute or two later—though some actually never returned, truth be known. When they did return, my husband would unknowingly twist the knife within them, saying, "In fact, we have four children."

Finally, I started pointing it out and asking them why they're making that face. "Oh?" they innocently respond, "What face?" When I explained the face that looks like they're going to be sick, they'd say "Oh, no, I feel fine," as if I'm imagining it.

Then, when the nurse came in to give me all the details of my tumor, the reason for "the faces" started to dawn on me. *Aggressive tumor, Stage III, Grade III, intensive treatment for a year, ongoing treatment likely for at least ten more years, node involvement, blah, blah, blah, scans and appointments all next week, six months of chemo to start ASAP* (and I won't even mention their foul talk of recurrence risk!) which reminds me...

In addition to "the face," I interrupt this regularly-scheduled program to share my experiences with "the face's" often partner-in-crime: "the words."

"We have never seen such dense breasts." Who knew my firm, perky rack would be a factor? If I had a dime for every time I heard how dense my breasts are, I could've paid all my cancer bills ten times over.

And, of course, "You're so fit and healthy," and "You have no modifiable risk factors." Meaning, I eat well, exercise regularly, don't drink alcohol, have been a vegetarian for twenty-five years, and have a twenty-five-year yoga and meditation practice. All of that translates in their minds into, "You're so low risk!" Yes, folks, my "low risk" landed me in Cancerland (My favorite comments throughout treatment were from different nurses and techs who asked if I was "an elite athlete." I'm not, but, even so, cancer doesn't discriminate, people!).

In the days that followed, various other versions continued to surface of "the face" and "the words" ("But you're so healthy! You do everything right!" Read: *If she got cancer, I'm completely fucked.*).

I call the next collective face experience, "student face" (though, the "fellow parent," "colleague," or "neighbor face" were all fair game, too).

The day I had received that fateful call from my doctor, I was on my way to teach a yoga philosophy class. I cancelled so that I could sit with my own feelings for a bit and call my husband, given this new reality. To make up for it, I agreed to meet with my students before my chemotherapy began. I had sent them an email, so they could digest my news privately and in their own time. That day, my dear friend Lizzie, also in the class, prepped them before my arrival: "Whatever you do, don't make 'the face.'" Some of them had to ask "What face?" Lizzie explained, "You know, the looking pitying and sick or horrified, making Kate feel like she has to apologize or take care of you."

Sure enough, before I was even seated, several students were already crying, and I looked out into a room full of "the face." I let them cry for a bit, and then, I had to put my foot down, letting them know that I know they care about me, are sad and scared and worried, maybe for me and maybe for themselves. But, after today, there's no more crying in front of me, or I'm cancelling class. While it did take some time, I was heartened to see that unlearning "the face" is, indeed, possible.

Perhaps, though, my favorite and all-time winner of "the face" award is "the inexperienced and scared-shitless new counselor face."

The weeks following my diagnosis were a blur of tests, scans, referrals, appointments, decisions, and procedures (hello, port!). Once I started chemo, the frequency and urgency of the appointments started to wane enough that I was able to attend to the less urgent, among them, a referral to the UCSF psycho-oncology department. While many of these appointments were not requested, I figured if UC offers and insurance pays, I'll give it a whirl—all in the name of healing, right? So, I made the appointment with a woman in their practice. "You'll love her," the scheduler cooed to me over the phone.

I arrived at the office and was handed a survey to complete that asked about my level of depression on a scale of one to five today, last week, in the last month; if I'm having trouble sleeping from said depression, doing daily tasks, sexual functioning, and so on, all about my assumed depression. Another page asked all the same questions about my presumed anxiety level. The third page asked about how many times I've thought about and/or tried to harm myself or another today, last week, in the last month.

Confused, I asked the person behind the desk, "What do I fill out if I'm not depressed?" She shrugged, "I don't really know."

The counselor came out to meet me at reception. She had "the face" on already as she approached me, all the way down the corridor and up to the front desk. I thought there was no way she could be the counselor—I'm only forty-four, but she looked like she was sixteen, on the first day of her first real job, *really* wanting to impress someone.

She introduced herself with a weak smile, and then said, "Oh, I see you haven't filled out your paperwork yet?"

"Oh, I have," I replied.

"But, they're all blank," she observed. Technically they weren't blank—I had filled out zeros where I could.

"I know, there's nothing for me to fill out."

"What do you mean?"

"I mean there's nothing for me to fill out."

She took the papers and looked through them quickly "So, you're not depressed?" she accused.

"No, I actually feel pretty good."

"Why are you here today?" she asked me, as we stood uncomfortably, still in the waiting area in front of the administrative staff and the other patients.

"Because I kept getting calls from your office about scheduling an appointment, so I kinda thought I should check it out and see if it's helpful." The admin staff behind the desk were on the edge of their seats, rarely getting this kind of treat to break the tedium of their day.

"Why don't you come with me to my office," she suggested. I obliged.

We sat down in her tiny, cramped office with no windows, and she gave me the worst version of "the face" that I have ever seen. She looked forced, strained. She was definitely trying very hard.

"So, let's get back to these papers, shall we? You're sure you're not depressed? You have *cancer*," she emphasized, almost pleading.

She then launched into a rehearsed speech about how much stress I must be under and how horrible it is having a cancer diagnosis. I tried to gently explain I have support from my twenty-five years working in the cancer world, and while I naturally feel worried or scared sometimes because I realize the severity of my situation or the gravity of my diagnosis, overall, I'm feeling pretty lucky to have all the support I do, my great medical team, and self-care skills. I'm doing everything I can.

Then, she cut me off and wheedled, "There's nothing that you're upset about or that's bothering you?"

"Well, actually there is one thing."

She shifted forward to the edge of her seat, her notebook and pencil at the ready, eagerly asking, "What?"

"The face."

"The face?"

"Yes, the face."

"What's the face?"

"You know, the pitying bullshit face that people give when they don't know how to respond authentically or are caught up in their own trip about my diagnosis, just like the one you're giving me now." I do my best imitation.

She fumbled her notebook, flustered, "My face?" she asked, incredulously.

"Yup," I smiled.

"I'm trying to look empathetic. Doesn't it seem like that to you?" she queried. Poor thing.

"Yes, it does seem like you're *trying* to look empathetic, but it doesn't look like you actually *are*. That's the problem," I told her, as kindly as I could.

And, then, "I truly believe you mean well, I wish you luck, and I won't be needing your services." I headed for the door and knew, happily, that I would never see the "the inexperienced and scared shitless new counselor face" again.

The "faces" still appeared from other directions though: those who reached out to tell me they had heard about my diagnosis from so-and-so (though, curiously, I had never heard anything from good ol' so-and-so), those who commented on my continuously changing appearance ("You look emaciated!" after I lost seven pounds and my ribs were protruding, but "Once you gain those same seven pounds back, you'll be fat again soon enough!"), and those acquaintances who, somehow, made it all about them.

To the latter, I ran into the wife of an old friend, who greeted me and then launched into how hard her life is, her house remodel, the contractor, how hard it is to get good help, and so on. As she was rambling on, I wondered if she knew about my diagnosis—her husband knew and surely he would've told her.

As I listened, I looked at her, I mean, really looked at her. Though she was polished and coifed, she looked terrible, sunken, drawn. I filled with a deep empathy for her, a crystal clarity of how hard her life *must* be, how truly she really *is* suffering. And, I felt so lucky to be me—cancer diagnosis, receiving chemo infusions each week, feeling like crap, worried about my kids and my future—than to be her, stuck as she was.

She broke through my thoughts and blurted, "Oh, well, I guess I should ask how *you* are?" Oh, so she *does* know. "I'm great!" I said, truthfully, "Started chemo, got my new Frankenstein-ian accessory," as I pulled down my shirt collar a little to reveal the port. She grimaced, then said, "Actually, I should ask you. I found a lump in my breast recently. Do you think it's cancer?"

"I have no idea."

"Well, can you feel it and tell me if it's cancer?"

"Uh, here?"

"Sure. Can you just feel it and tell me if mine feels like cancer to you?"

"Uh, I found my own lump because I give myself regular exams and I know my own breast tissue well, but I couldn't even tell if mine was cancer or not—I called my doctor right away and had a biopsy. Even my doctor who felt it couldn't tell from feeling if it was cancerous or not."

"Can't you just feel it and tell me?" an impatient, pleading in her voice.

"We're in the middle of a restaurant, and even if I felt it, I would have no idea if it was cancer or not."

She was visibly disappointed in me. I did not give her what she wanted, some kind of assurance.

I bid her good bye and good luck, encouraged her to follow up with her doctor, and gracefully exited the building.

I feel such empathy for the suffering so many of us put ourselves through, and truly never have felt luckier just to be me, with all my imperfections, my fat and my emaciated ribs, my ugly and painful port, cancerous cells, my sweet, beautiful children and husband, my amazing circle of friends and those I love and laugh with deeply, each of them with "the exquisite, present and generous face." The best kind of face there is.

II. BODY TRAUMA

"Pain is the doorway to the here and now. Physical or emotional pain is an ultimate form of ground, saying, to each of us, in effect, there is no other place than this place, no other body than this body, no other limb or joint or pang or sharpness or heartbreak but this searing presence."

— David Whyte, "Pain" from *Consolations: The Solace, Nourishment and Underlying Meaning of Everyday Words*

Lights, Camera, Action!

Laurie Hessen Pomeranz

The phone call came from Missy, in Talent Acquisition. She explained that she represented a medical entertainment TV show in Los Angeles. They were interested in featuring our new Bay Area Young Survivors anthology, *The Day My Nipple Fell Off*, in an episode about breast cancer. The title story of the book was my story, so she called me. The story told the tale of my nipple falling off, after what was billed as a "nipple-sparing mastectomy." Of course, there's always the odd chance of a weird complication, but you never think that will be *your* weird complication.

I told Missy that I was sure that our editor and fellow author, Erin Williams Hyman, and I would love to come down and appear on the show.

We exchanged information, and I hung up to call Erin and let her know what I'd just signed us up for. She was ecstatic. We were giddy. TV! Recognition of our newly published book! We had dreamt of getting on *Ellen* or *Oprah*. This was close enough to get us started!

We imagined the fabulous night out we'd have in LA. There would be cocktails. Pool time. Girl time. Beauty sleep. King-sized beds. No kids. We imagined the scene in hair and make-up, getting camera-ready. Then, show time. Repping for our cancer sisters! Putting faces to young survivors!

I called Missy back to let her know we were in. She said, "We are just wrapping up our planning for this episode. I'll call you back with the plans once they are finalized, K?"

Missy called me the next day, and said that she was really sorry, but they had decided to devote the breast cancer episode to the BRCA gene, because of the recent Angelina Jolie-inspired awareness of the BRCA mutation, which can lead to an increased risk of breast and ovarian cancer.

Missy said that they would love to keep our numbers and call us for a future episode. I said, "Sure, please keep us in mind! Just wondering, what kind of episode might you have us on?" Without missing a beat, Missy replied, "Well, you know, sometimes we do shows about, you know, like something embarrassing happened to my boob, or my butt, or something." I imagined she was snapping her gum and twirling her hair around her finger.

I'm speechless. How dare she say that what happened to me is "embarrassing?" And how dare she assume that I am embarrassed?

Long pause.

I told Missy that on second thought, this wouldn't be a good fit and we would not be interested in appearing on a future episode, after all.

I called Erin and told her what happened. I said we would just have to plan our own girls' weekend in LA.

We never got to LA, or on TV, before Erin died. But, we did share a deliciously mojito-soaked afternoon in a hot tub in Palm Springs, with our scars and our misshapen and missing boobs.

If we were supposed to be feeling embarrassed, we never got the memo.

She Stuffs It Down

Allison B.

Two years
Since both breasts,
Ovaries,
Tubes
Vanished.

Stabbing pain,
Emptiness.
Scars reflecting back.
I am lost.
Am I even a woman anymore?

Foreign objects invade me.
Cold.
Hard.

My body is not my own.
Bumps.
Holes.

My femininity, stolen.

No choice.

Doctor after doctor insisted.

What if they were wrong?

What if it didn't spread?

What if the BRCA mutation would never take me?

It's fucking barbaric

This "treatment."

Did I make the right choice?

I'll never know.

And now I'm left

Disfigured,

Horrified each time I pass the mirror.

I don't recognize myself.

I have become someone else

I am outside, watching

As she stuffs it down,

This other me.

She's supposed to be ok.

They need her to be ok.

That sweet little face tilted up with hopeful eyes.
That tender caregiver desperate to have his lover back.
That sister who still cries for our mother lost.
That father who laments passing down this gene.
That colleague feeling lost without a captain.

They need her to be ok.

So she smiles.
She holds her head high.
Her heart cries.

The incisions mend.
The scars run deeper.
Piercing pain.

And she carries on.

My Soul is Burning

Janet S.

My soul is burning. Inside, a hot coal in the middle of my body. It's killing the tumors there, in my soul. It hurts, it burns. I don't want to feel it. I writhe in pain, in circles around myself, trying to kill the hot brick in my soul, probably the best way to cool off the tumors without killing me. It doesn't feel good. I want to stop caring about the burning and stop feeling in my soul.

New Year, New Me?

Andrea Ghoorah Sieminski

January 1, 2013

Well, the day came. I knew it would, but it was still shocking as hell for me.

Exactly two weeks after my first chemo infusion, my hair started falling out in clumps. For the twenty-four hours prior to it actually falling out, my hair *ached*. You know how it feels after you've had your hair in a tight ponytail for hours? That's the feeling I'm talking about.

So, I decided to shave my head today—New Year's Day. Something about the timing felt symbolic. I wanted to end 2012 with a full head of hair, and then, in 2013, get on with it and kick cancer's ass.

My husband Paul and I filled our day with errands and a movie, neither of us bringing up the task that remained—buzzing off all my hair. Like many women, my hairstyle is part of my identity. Shaving my hair off is like losing my security blanket. Will people act uncomfortable around me? Being bald will announce to the world that I'm "sick." Paul keeps telling me that it's all bullshit. He tells me that shaving my head is bad-ass and announces to the world that I'm fighting cancer. It's nothing to be ashamed of. Just the opposite, in fact. "Wear it proudly," he tells me. "So what if you look different? You are different. And stronger, and wiser and tougher."

At 7pm, I couldn't wait any longer. Paul set up a barber shop of sorts in our bathroom, and, there I stood, naked, with his electric clippers in hand. Paul gave me another really good pep talk and assured me that I'm beautiful no matter what and encouraged me to go for it. To hype me up, he even downloaded that scene from *GI Jane* where Demi Moore shaves her head (It didn't have the intended effect). It took me several false starts, but then I finally went in for the kill.

I was crying the entire time. I wish that I felt liberated and strong and had a "fuck-you-cancer" attitude. But, I didn't. I wept through it and then handed the clippers over to Paul to let him finish the parts I couldn't bear.

He is the best husband in the world. He worked swiftly, reminding me that I'm beautiful, that this means the medicine is working, the cancer will get killed and my hair will grow back. He was so supportive, acting as my knees when my own were buckling.

So, the deed was done, and I was feeling miserable for myself. I got into bed and cried under the covers. After a while, I decided to stop my pity party and try to eat something. I made some pasta, and not ten minutes later, I puked everything up and cried some more.

January 2, 2013

Today is a new day, and I'm off to my second of sixteen chemotherapy sessions. Once this infusion is completed, I'll be halfway through with the Adriamycin-Cytoxin portion of the protocol.

Trying to be glass half full today. But, it's hard…being bald hasn't turned me into GI Jane overnight.

Hair, Hair

Laura Pexton

Hair, hair, it's everywhere.

On your pillow and on the floor,

Touch your head, there's a handful more.

All over your house and on your clothes,

Into the garbage it will go.

In the shower and down the drain,

Efforts to keep it are all in vain.

Desperate, you want to cry.

At last it's the clippers you must try.

Clip clip. Snip snip.

Buzz buzz. Sniff sniff.

In the mirror you sorrowfully stare,

A bewildered bald stranger greets you there.

A noggin so obvious, so shiny, so white,

Without lustrous locks it just doesn't look right.

Now time to find a wig to wear.

Shall it be dark or light or curly hair?

Long or short, blonde or straight,

"Whatever you choose, you'll look just great!"

Eventually your new hair will grow.

The color, the texture you just don't know.

A little or lots, thick or thin,

Hooray! It's finally growing back in.

There's one more thing I want to say,

A reminder to think of everyday;

Be grateful you're alive and you.

Remember there's so much good you can do.

Always remember that HAIR IS GREAT.

So enjoy your hair for goodness sake!

Bury You

Allison B.

Where are you?

Where are my beautiful breasts?

In a drain somewhere, I suppose

You've died

But where is the funeral?

I killed you

I'm scared of you

How can I be

the murderer and the victim?

Part of me died

I miss you

I'm sorry

I love you

I'm sorry

I'm sorry

I'm sorry

If I bury you in my heart
will you become part of my heart?
Will you live on
and become something new?
Something beautiful again?

Will the pain
stop twisting
pulling
piercing?

Afraid
afraid of myself

I can't trust you
you betrayed me
I was fine over here on the right
the left one had the cancer.

You blindsided me
How can I ever trust you again?

Let me lie down with you

behind you

holding you

I'm sorry

I'm sorry

I'm so very sorry

Curl up in my embrace.

I love you

I love you

I love you

Until We Let Go

Janet S.

Act 1

Scene 1

Background music: MIA's lyrics from Bad Girls, "Live fast, die young. Bad girls do it well." As pain meds kick in, music fades to Billy Joel's Captain Jack, "Captain Jack will get you high tonight. And take you to your special island."

JANET   Hey, Body, let's face it. You started this.

BODY   Yes, and if you'd leave me alone we'd be peacefully dead by now. But you keep poisoning me, cutting parts off, and now this radiation. And you complain, "It hurts, stop doing this to me, Body!" And I say, "You're doing it to yourself." Leave me alone, and we'd pass gently and quietly into the night.

JANET   True statements. But, I love our life, don't you?

53

BODY   Some of your ideas of fun are extreme and painful.
            I'd prefer more yoga, long walks, not mountain
            climbs and heli-skiing. More massages, dancing, and
            talks.

JANET   Yeah, we don't talk much. And I do push you. But, is
            it so bad that you want out right now?

BODY   I don't have much choice. Cancer is all-consuming.
            It's gonna kill us eventually.

            Up to you how much poison, radiation, and surgery
            you want to suffer through.

            But, I'd request more pain meds at the very least—
            we don't have to suffer quite so much. You're always
            too proud, too strong, "I can take this." You say,
            "Body, it's ok to puke, but can you just wait thirty
            minutes for the pain meds to kick in?" Mixed
            messages, Janet.

JANET   I want to Do, See, Touch, Taste, Feel, Smell, and
            Experience everything! Don't you, Body?

BODY   As long as we can, and it's nice, then yes. But, we can't do everything. We all have to end sometime. There will always be things undone. You're in such a rush!

JANET   You aren't giving me much time.

BODY   Lighten up, it's ok not to finish everything. Most people don't experience half of what you've already done in life. Be thankful. Enjoy our friends, love, sunny days, blizzards. Take what comes and enjoy it. Until we let go and die.

         I hope we don't keep fighting each other to the end.

JANET   Me too. I'm listening to you. It's just hard to swallow.

III. RECONSTRUCTION

"You can go just an inch.
You can mark your progress breath by breath."

— Cheryl Strayed, *Tiny Beautiful Things: Advice on Love and Life from Dear Sugar*

Like Sexting...But Not Really

Robin Bruns Worona

It's 10:45 on a sunny Saturday morning. I'm in my bedroom with the door locked, logged into a videochat program. Waiting.

Suddenly, an older man with white hair and a full mustache appears on the screen. He is sitting on a couch in front of some bookshelves. Not exactly what I expected, but ok. We chat casually for a moment before he says, "Ok, let's take a look." I lift my shirt, I have already unclasped my bra, and place my phone as close to my right breast as I can. I laugh self-consciously. "Hold the phone still so it can focus," he says, followed after a moment by "Ok." I pull my shirt down and point the camera back to my face.

I wait, trying not to giggle or blush, for the old man to say something. It is my tendency in these situations to introduce humor, but sometimes that only makes things more awkward. He clears his throat, "It does not look infected to me," he says.

I breathe a sigh of relief.

Fifteen minutes ago, I texted (or, I guess I technically sexted) a picture of my boob to my best friend, a doctor. That is also what she said, but two opinions are always better than one, right?

The man floating on the phone screen in front of me continues, "Just keep it clean and open to the air. I'll call in a prescription for you just in case it gets worse tomorrow, but I don't think it will."

Uh, open to the air? I'm supposed to go to a four-year-old's birthday party today. Does he suggest I go topless? I keep my mouth shut and thank him.

I was worried. When I took off the steri-strips, the tape for my wounds, before my shower this morning, there was an area that seemed red and oozy. The old me would have said, "Oh, it's fine. I'll call the doc if it gets worse." But since my diagnosis, I have lost faith in that approach.

I felt that lump for a few months before I went to get it checked. Not that it made much of a difference. They told me that tumor was growing for seven to ten years. But, I keep thinking that the next time it might really matter. So, every new symptom now is a struggle. Call now? Wait? Jump up? Sit down? Run? Walk? Of course, I always seem to get these symptoms on the weekends, or when my plastic surgeon is in Belgium.

I only arrived at the video-chat-doctor after forty-five minutes on the phone with a nurse who kept asking me ridiculous questions, like, "Does it hurt?" So I had to explain to her, a nurse, that after one has had a mastectomy, one no longer has any sensation in that breast, even after reconstruction. "It LOOKS like it hurts," I said, and gave her the finger. She was thankfully NOT on video chat.

I fiddle with my phone for a few minutes, trying to be sure I have deleted the picture of my ravaged breast. My friend was having lunch with her mother, who I've known since high school, when I texted her the picture. I hope she did not show her mother. I imagined them, sitting at some sunny, white-tablecloth brunch spot, ogling my excreting stitches. Ridiculous, of course. She wouldn't do that. I hope she has deleted the picture. I hope that her phone is not stolen or forgotten in the bathroom. I wish I could make that picture self-destruct.

Rebellious Boob

Kristen Zeitzer

I thought you were beautiful
I thought you were nice
Until you tried to escape

My surgeon made a charming home for you
Inside my body
I took care to welcome you

Only two months later
You opened me
And started to leave

You look black from the outside
To cover you again
We had to make your room smaller

So please stay home
Safe, sound, and perky
A little longer

Send in the Leeches

Meaghan Calcari Campbell

My eyes opened and closed, lids heavy, mind tuning in and out to the beeps of the various hospital machines. Surgery was over. I was in recovery.

My throat was sore and dry from the intubation. I told the nurse my mouth was the Sahara. Like, really, I was sure my mouth had transformed into a parched, lifeless and dusty desert (if I told her once, I might have told her twenty times. Ok, forty times). She could only give me a few ice cubes at a time though, as she hurriedly moved among the patients in the recovery bay.

Then, the shivers started. I had a reaction to the anesthesia that caused intense hypothermia-like jitters and jaw rattling. My bleary mind wondered, "How can my mouth be the Sahara and my body be the Arctic?" The nurse inserted a drug into my IV to relax my muscles.

Next, the *itchies* started. The reaction to the morphine caused tickles and prickles all over, hopscotching across my body—the arch of my right foot, my left butt cheek, my right ear lobe. The nurse inserted another drug into my already-loaded IV to solve this problem.

64

When I could start drinking water, I gulped it too fast, got the hiccups, and started throwing up.

My husband Mike and I joked that I was plowing through the ten plagues. In my anesthesia fog though, I was having trouble remembering the name of that "L" insect that was supposed to swarm in.

Over a year before waking up in this recovery room, right after I finished chemotherapy for breast cancer, and before I started radiation, I had a mastectomy. During that surgery, they placed a temporary implant that the surgeon would slowly expand to make room for an eventual silicone implant. I would need another surgery to swap the temporary fix for the real deal, er, silicone implant.

So, I scheduled that swap surgery, and all went smoothly. My recovery marched along as it should, hitting milestones, gaining my range of motion back, lifting one, two, and then three pound weights. Life started to flow back into my life.

Except, at eight weeks post-operation, on a sunny Sunday, I was changing clothes and noticed blood in my bra. Weird. So, I peeked at my breast. It was red and hot, angry.

What unfolded was an emergency phone call to the surgeon, a Sunday evening visit to the deserted clinic, a surgery scheduled the next morning to remove the infected implant, and a prescription for intensive antibiotics to prevent sepsis. Radiation treatment had thinned my skin, making my incision split. I knew this failure and infection were more likely with my radiated skin, but really, eight weeks after surgery, I thought I was in the clear.

I was heartbroken. This was supposed to have been my final surgery, putting breast cancer in my rearview mirror. Now, I would need at least two more surgeries if I wanted to have a breast, or even some semblance of a breast.

I'm thirty-four. I wear v-neck shirts. Swim. Travel for work. I do not want people to stare at a lopsided chest, silently judging, wondering if I was born like this, deformed, or what trauma took my breast. Nor do I want to be saddled with a prosthetic breast, trying to remember where it is, what suitcase it ended up in, whether it got lodged in the washing machine. I wanted a breast as much as it can be wanted. I resolved to dig deeply, and signed up for the next surgeries.

A week after the failed temporary implant was removed and infection cleared, I went back in for the big gun surgery, a latissimus flap. The surgical team would take part of my latissimus back muscle, tissue and skin, and thread it through my armpit, adding it to my breast. They would also excise the breast skin that was no longer viable. It sounded so clinical. Viable, viva, life, alive. My breast skin was the opposite of that—dead.

In pre-op, the surgical team drew all over my torso, chest, and back. They said most of the lines were for landmarks, but it gave me a sense of what was to come, as I peered down at my criss-crossed body. The fragmentation on my body was like looking into

66

a funhouse mirror.

When starting my IV, the nurse asked if I wanted lidocaine to help numb the process. Feeling strong-willed, I declined. Then the first two IV attempts nosedived, and my overused vein exploded. I passed out because of the pain and discomfort.

We were off to a tremendous start.

Coming back to the post-op recovery room, and after clearing the hurdles of a dry mouth, shivers, itchies, and vomiting, things were starting to settle down. I got into an easy rhythm with the nurses, the bedpan, hospital food on demand, and that patient-controlled morphine.

The big unveiling came the next day. When the surgical team cleared away the bandages, I inhaled and directed my eyes downward. All that hospital pudding in my stomach started to make its way back up my throat. The scene horrified me. It was like having a mastectomy again. Losing a body part again. The post-op landscape of my chest looked like a B-movie version of Frankenstein's monster. Multiple zig-zag incisions. Purple, swollen, marred skin. Deep maroon, caked blood.

And, what's this my eyes shift to next? What is this black dot on my breast now? It's a mole. From my back. Oh-my-fucking-god-I'm-a-science-experiment. The skin they removed from my back had a constellation of moles on it. They now live on my new breast. If I ever wondered what my back looked like, I have my answer.

One of my favorite Maya Angelou quotes surfaced in my mind: "I've learned that you can tell a lot about a person by the way he/she handles these three things: a rainy day, lost luggage, and tangled Christmas tree lights." I'd humbly add the latissimus flap surgery. So, after a brief mental pep talk that maybe the worst was over now, I looked up, hopeful, back to my surgeon.

His face told me something else.

The surgical team was worried that my body wasn't flowing enough blood through the remodeled tissue. The words "necrosis" and "dead" floated through the air like bubbles that I immediately wanted to stab.

The surgeon said there was one last trick up his sleeve if blood flow didn't return: leeches.

Leeches?

Leeches.

Leeches?

Yes, leeches. They do a great job pulling blood to a surgical site. In fact, they do such an A+ job that I would also need a blood transfusion afterwards.

I'm a nature girl. I live in California. I like trees and animals and oceans. I love the idea of looking to nature for solutions. But, are you fucking kidding me that the best we've got are blood-sucking worms?

That "L" insect I couldn't remember that was part of the plagues? Well, it came to me. Locusts.

But, leeches would probably count too.

Both Sides Now

Ann Kim

I shuffled from my bedroom into the bathroom, my eyes still bleary with sleep. I pulled my nightgown up over my head, turned on the shower, and waited for the water to heat up before stepping into the tub. I drew the shower curtain and closed my eyes, allowing the hot water to soak into my hair and skin and the steam to fill my nostrils. With my eyes still closed, I reached for the soft, white bar of soap and began to lather my arms, my shoulders, my breasts. And then I opened my eyes, looked down, and yelled, "Honey!"

I rinsed off quickly, hopped out of the tub, and wrapped myself in a towel. I yelled again, this time more loudly, with greater urgency, "Honey!"

"What?" my husband asked, groggy and unaccustomed to being bellowed at so early in the morning.

I stood before him, my wet hair dripping down my face, and opened up my towel like a flasher to an unsuspecting victim.

"Do you notice anything unusual?" I asked.

"Oh my God, it's a raisin," he replied.

Indeed, my right breast did bear a striking resemblance to a raisin, although I thought a more apt comparison would have been to the free helium balloon that the nice grocer had given to my young son earlier that week: round, firm and joyful one day; deflated, wrinkly and sad the next.

"What happened?" my husband asked.

"I think my boob exploded."

Contracture is not a word that most people use in their everyday lives. It's not even a word that most people know the meaning of. For those not well-versed in breast cancer lingo: imagine your stereotypical bleached-blonde B-list actress with boobs so unnaturally spherical and shiny that you think, "Ouch, that's gotta be uncomfortable." That's contracture.

I remember the first time I heard the word. My cancer surgeon and I had decided that a unilateral mastectomy would be the most effective way to deal with the three tumors in my right breast, and I was talking with the plastic surgeon about reconstruction options. After agreeing on a saline implant, the plastic surgeon began to describe the litany of potential complications, including the possibility of contracture. I remember tuning him out. It was like listening to the teacher in the *Peanuts* cartoon—wah, wah, wah-wah-wah—or, more accurately, like the legal disclaimer at the end of a Viagra commercial. Contracture is the four-hour erection of breast reconstruction.

In their natural state, breasts are soft and round and have a lovely little droop that is both pleasing to the eye and touch, as well as obedient to the laws of gravity. After my mastectomy, my plastic surgeon did a wonderful job of creating a natural-looking mate to my intact, disease-free left breast. My breasts weren't identical—"they're meant to be sisters, not twins," is how one doctor described it—but they were a well-matched pair.

A few months after my surgery, however, I noticed that my right breast was changing. It was getting firmer. It was losing some of its droop. It was starting to defy gravity. I went to my plastic surgeon to ask him what was going on.

"Well, I told you about the risk of contracture," he said, looking disappointed. Yes, he had. Wah, wah, wah-wah-wah.

I went through another surgery. The plan was to remove the scar tissue that had built up around my saline implant and caused the contracture, and to replace the old implant with a brand-new one. At first, the sisters were once again a dynamic duo, but after a few weeks, I saw the tell-tale signs of contracture again: firmness, perkiness, gravity-defiance. I know most forty-year-old women would kill to have boobs that could be described as firm and perky, but it's not so great when one boob points south and the other points due north.

My plastic surgeon practically begged to do another surgery, but he couldn't provide me any assurance that the contracture wouldn't return, and I didn't want to go under the knife again. I went to a physical therapist and tried massaging the scar tissue so that it would soften, but to little avail. After a while, I just reconciled myself to having uneven boobs and wearing loose-fitting tops, which I did for a couple years.

Then, it happened. The infamous shower scene. The Raisin Incident. The Day My Boob Exploded.

My poor plastic surgeon. When I showed up at his office and flashed him my shriveled raisin, I don't know what was more deflated: my former helium balloon of a boob or the look on his face.

"I can fix it," he offered.

"No," I said. "I'm sorry, but I can't do this anymore. I'm done trying."

He looked sad. I felt like we were breaking up.

My plastic surgeon performed yet another surgery, this time to remove my ruptured implant, leaving me with a noticeable depression in my chest that I dubbed "Crater Lake." He wrote me a prescription for a breast prosthesis. And then, we said goodbye.

The sweet lady at Nordstrom provided me with a peach-colored, gel-filled prosthesis to match my 34-C left breast. For a few years, I lived happily with that prosthesis, making sure to insert it into my pocketed mastectomy bra every morning before getting dressed.

One day, I found a lump in my hitherto disease-free, intact left breast. Mild panic ensued. The biopsy came back negative; the lump was benign. Unbeknownst to my poor left breast, however, I had instituted a zero tolerance policy in the years since my cancer diagnosis. I decided to have a prophylactic contralateral mastectomy. For those not well-versed in breast cancer lingo, that means I decided to cut off my otherwise-healthy left boob.

When I went back to that sweet lady at Nordstrom to say that I needed two new prostheses, she asked if I wanted my old 34-C boobs or if I wanted to go bigger.

"No," I said. "I want to go smaller."

"You want to go smaller?" she asked incredulously.

"Yeah, I want yoga boobs."

"Yoga boobs?"

"Yeah, yoga boobs," I explained. "Boobs that a dancer would have. Boobs that won't give me a black eye if I go jogging."

She went to the storeroom and brought me the smallest prostheses she could find, along with a pretty, flirty bra that had discreet prosthesis pockets.

I slipped on my new boobs. They were soft, round, and had a lovely little droop.

Boyle's Law

Deborah Cohan

I arrived in Cusco, Peru on the first day of my trip—breathless and exhausted at 11,000 feet. My newly-anointed boyfriend and I planned this romantic getaway, to be part of my process in moving beyond my cancer. Instead of the anticipated bliss, my dominant sensation was the loud and continuous crinkling in both of my breasts whenever I lifted my arms, rotated my torso or touched my chest. It was a potent reminder that my breasts are synthetic and not a natural part of my body. I worried that perhaps they expanded so much that they were leaking, with the sudden gain in elevation.

I contacted my otherwise brilliant oncologist who, it turns out, had never heard of altitude-associated implant expansion. I emailed my little situation to my always-helpful support group, the Bay Area Young Survivors. Almost instantly, and from two time-zones away, I received multiple emails from my breast friends, sharing their own version of the same experience, while skiing in Colorado or scaling mountains in northern California.

Even though I was no longer anxious, I had a lingering unease. I did not want a reminder—while on vacation, a romantic vacation, no less—of what was an ambivalent decision two years ago today to undergo reconstruction.

But, like all good life lessons, this odd somatic sensation persisted and gave me the opportunity to fully milk this breast situation. I reflected on the original surgical decision and my exploration of vanity. I reflected on my anger that there are no biological implants (I want mine made out of mushrooms and seaweed!). I reflected on the cruel irony of toxic medical waste created by most conventional cancer treatments. I reflected on how, despite so much time spent reflecting and dancing and drawing and talking and healing, I clearly had not yet moved on and "my" breasts were still not "mine."

A few days later, I began my hike to Machu Picchu, and, while at 15,000 feet, my breasts became comically louder, and noticeably bigger. The degree of the crinkling matched the degree of my breathlessness, and I wondered if this would become my new normal. My boyfriend was, in the meantime, getting a quick education in implants.

We returned a few days later to Cusco, coming down 4,000 feet, and I noticed how, unlike the week prior, I could climb steep stairs to the Incan ruins without losing my breath. And, my breasts were no longer crinkling. Just like my heart and lungs, my breasts had acclimated to the altitude. And, for the first time, my breast implants felt like they were truly a part of me.

My Nipples Are Fading

Marla Stein

My breasts, once lopsided and uneven, to the extent of being
faltered
Today, they are balanced and forever altered.

Before they were implants, they were heavy and frumpy;
Now they are perky, but still quite lumpy.

My nipples, though formally bright, are now currently light;
They lack sensation, but are still quite a sight.

They used to serve a purpose and have wonderfully natural
shading;
My reality now is that my tattooed nipples are fading.

Every few years, they're tweaked with my color of choosing;
The fun of survivorship allows for this musing.

While it's still challenging, at times, to embrace my present look
All effort to feel feminine remains the goal of this work.

Window Shopping

Rebecca J. Hogue

My husband Scott and I often find ourselves laughing at things that are absurd, but real, nonetheless. I recognize it clearly for what it is: a necessary coping mechanism. But, I'm also aware of how easily something funny can turn into something sad.

When I was an undergraduate, one of my friends had a recurrence of cancer. At her wedding shower, while she was sitting with the news that her cancer had come back, we were laughing about this or that—things that women laugh at during wedding showers, like ridiculous wedding shower presents and cringe-worthy shower games—and the focus of the jokes turned to wigs. There was laughing at first, but then, a sudden transition to tears. This is what I'm aware of every time I laugh about something. I'm aware that at any moment, that laugh can become a cry.

Today's laugh was about prosthetic breasts. I just learned there are special prosthetic breasts for swimming—aquadynamic breasts! They even make aerodynamic prosthetic breasts. Who knew? I was reminded of Aimee Mullins TED talk, "My 12 pairs of legs." Aimee talks about how having various prosthetic legs allows her to be different heights. She talks about legs as things that allow her to have superpowers. For example, when she wants to run fast, she has special legs for that. I was laughing as my mind raced—if I don't opt for reconstruction from my breast cancer surgery, then I, too, could have multiple sets of prosthetics for multiple purposes! I could have bigger breasts to fill out my favorite shirt, or smaller ones when I want to appear less noticeable. Then, of course, it occurs to me, that people who saw me regularly would find it rather odd that my chest size kept changing. And, how would I go clothes shopping? Which breasts would I wear? And, if I were to get into competitive swimming, would the breasts I choose to wear affect how fast I swim? And would that be considered cheating?

As I wade into the morass of breast cancer surgical decision-making, I am exploring my options. Reconstruction means more surgery, more complicated surgery, and more healing time. No reconstruction means a life of prosthetics.

Scott and I went for a walk around Sausalito on Saturday. I realized that I was looking at other women's breasts. I had never really taken notice of other women's breasts before, but, now, I find myself drawn to them. I am looking. I'm not even sure what I'm thinking when I'm looking, but I am certainly finding myself looking. I laugh, then I swallow tears. Prosthetics or not, I find myself window shopping.

IV. RELATIONSHIPS

"When did we see each other face to face? Not until you saw into my cracks and I saw into yours. Before that we were just looking at ideas of each other, like looking at your window shade, but never seeing inside. But once the vessel cracks, the light can get in. The light can get out."

— John Green, *Paper Towns*

Somewhere Down the Line

Meaghan Calcari Campbell

"All this talk about eggs has me hungry," I muse to myself as we hustle between the reproductive endocrinologist's office and the exam room, where I'm handed a stack of flimsy tissue paper that magically becomes a flimsy tissue paper gown. Voilà!

The doctor enters and instructs me, "One footsie here, one footsie there," to get my feet into the stirrups. My husband Mike stands stoically by my side, or actually, more like by my head. This stirrup thing is new territory for him. We are going to count my eggs to see how many viable ones are left. If the eggs are a-plenty, maybe, just maybe, there is time, before I start chemo, to harvest and fertilize eggs, then pop the embryos into a seismically-retrofitted freezer somewhere in San Francisco for safe-keeping. An insurance policy, a fertility preservation literally frozen in time and space, a "just in case" I lose my fertility after chemo and hormone therapies and, oh, menopause at age thirty-two. And, also because people with cancer aren't always "ideal adoptive parents," according to the psychologist we meet with, who coaches us through this decision-making and keeping our marriage intact under stress.

Um, how the hell did we get here?

It was less than twenty-four hours ago that the blood rushed out of my extremities and up my torso to my neck and cheeks. I looked at Mike, sitting there, mouth agape, as still as 3am in suburbia.

"It's cancer."

"We're sure we didn't mix up the lab results."

"Fast-growing."

"Unknown prognosis."

"I set up appointments with the oncologist, surgeon, and a reproductive endocrinologist starting tomorrow."

"Oh, that big long name means fertility doctor."

"Well, because assuming you need chemotherapy, you could be left infertile."

"Here's a tissue."

"And a hand-sewn, stuffed heart to squeeze, especially after your surgery."

"I'm so sorry."

"They can validate your parking at the front desk."

And, so, here we are.

Without knowing if I'm even going to live through this cancer diagnosis, we're talking about having children, assuming we even want children, and our *own* children at that. We're talking about if I die, what we'll do with the embryos, and if he dies, what we'll do with the embryos, and if we get divorced, what we'll do with the embryos, and if there is a nuclear war…you get the picture.

We are both thirty-two, freshly married and new homeowners, worried less about reproducing and more about filling our house with friends, graduating beyond Ikea furniture manuals, and racking up airline miles to get to our next international sojourn. We were a bit later getting married than many of our friends. We share joy with those friends who are matriculating into first and even second-time parenthood. But, we have not felt pressure to speed up any decision-making for us about whether to parent, or not to parent.

I never grew up dreaming about becoming a mother. You know that image of a little girl, swinging around a baby doll, cooing in a sing-song voice, practicing for when she becomes a real mom? Not me.

Mike coached and mentored kids through college and gets juice from hanging out with them, always assuming he would become a father. You know that image of the All-American boy who grows up to become a strapping man with a fluffy little towhead on his shoulders? That's Mike.

Sure, I taught and tutored through college. I love my nieces and nephew. But me, a mother? Childbirth terrifies me—there's the growing a person in my belly, being responsible for that person's every ounce of well-being, and seeing that person emerge from my body intact, while keeping my body intact. Mostly, though, I think about Elizabeth Stone's quote describing motherhood, "It is to decide forever to have your heart go walking around outside your body," and how utterly fragile it would all be, that I would become bowled over with emotion, my heart breaking every minute. Adoption sounds, on the pregnancy and childbirth angles, like a less frightening option if I needed one. However, Mike prefers having our own biological children, if we were able to.

Before our wedding, now a year ago, we were at a standstill on the topic but wanted to give ourselves an answer before the "I do's" were exchanged. So, Mike committed that he would stick with me if I never came around to wanting children, and we both committed to kicking the kid decision further down the line.

Totally workable.

Except that now, we are down the line.

Sort of.

After my breast cancer diagnosis and the blitzkrieg of doctors' appointments and blood draws and biopsies and scans and insomniac nights spent awake crying and talking and crying, we decided to go for it. To harvest my eggs, freeze those embryos, and figure the rest out later. Even further down the line. We don't know if this fast-growing cancer in my body is going to kill me this year, or next year, or in twenty-five years, or ever.

Meanwhile, each year, when the annual "embryo storage fee" comes due, I write a check and think about it as an investment in a nursery, albeit a very barren, icy nursery, the "Just in Case" nursery. And, as I regularly drive on a street that hugs the San Francisco Bay, I wave hello to our eleven embryos, our totsicles, tucked away in their earthquake-safe freezer, and scheme about getting Mike eleven onesies, or eleven Christmas stockings to hang on the mantle, or maybe just eleven lottery tickets. Because I'm still here and alive, down the line.

Cancer Baby

Sara Mahdavi

On the day of my first chemotherapy infusion, I sat in the chair at my oncologist's office, waiting for them to pump chemicals into the port that was connected to a vein to my heart. I gazed out at a view of the San Francisco Bay. It brought me right back to my pregnancy with my son, Nikan, now a loving, charismatic three-year-old. He was so comfortable in utero that I had to be induced. I refused—twice—and signed a form acknowledging this could result in "fetal death." At that time, I fully trusted my body to do what was best to get through this, surely helped along by foot massages, acupuncture, spicy foods, and long, uphill walks. After these still did not jumpstart my contractions, I finally returned to the hospital—the weight of potential "fetal death" hanging over me—to succumb to the induction. I thought—wrongly, it turned out!—that induction would prevent the epidural-free, natural birth I wanted. In the birthing room, I sat at the window, overlooking that stunning view of the San Francisco Bay.

Flash forward to my first chemo infusion, and I was looking at the same view and asking myself the same questions as during my induction: why is this happening? How could this be? Wait, is this actually happening? But, this time, I had <u>no</u> trust in my body and no idea what would happen to me—would I have an allergic reaction to the drugs? What side effects would I have? Would it leak into and damage my surrounding tissue? And, most of all, would it even work? The sadness, anxiety, anger and fear washed over me again.

It struck me: this whole cancer experience was like having a baby, too!*[1]

Just as with pregnancy, I was avoiding bourbon, sushi, and sick people. And missing them in that order.

Nausea and fatigue are side-effects of both chemo and pregnancy. To combat them, I went to yoga and acupuncture, meditated, and tried guided imagery and affirmations. All these things to help my body and mind through the natural birth, I mean, cancer treatment. There were special yoga classes for people like me—yoga for pregnant mamas, yoga for new mamas, yoga for cancer patients. Bonus: cancer yoga is much cheaper than pregnant or new mama yoga, and sometimes it's even free!

Speaking of free, you get free shit as a new mom *and* as a cancer patient. Free nursing cover, diapers, and Aquaphor. Free

---

*Well, except that instead of growing an amazing, beautiful little being, I was trying to eradicate gremlin cancer cells. And, while I had nine months to prepare for birth, cancer hit me like a ton of bricks.

wig, hair wrap, make up, taxi vouchers, and, for radiation treatment, Manuka honey in place of Aquaphor!

I even looked pregnant during chemo. People—particularly those who have not been through chemo recently, or ever—told me to eat as much as I could, assuming I would have nausea and food aversions and become a waif. But, every person reacts differently, and treatment has come a long way. I got an IV drip of anti-nausea medication right before the chemo drip, plus Benadryl, Pepcid, and a steroid. So instead of wasting away, because of the pre-meds, I spent my infusions eating through the oncologist's office. I packed little feasts—crackers, oranges, apples, almonds, pistachios—and would eat them ALL. I also hydrated like an elephant to flush out the chemicals and keep my liver healthy, so, naturally, I had to pee constantly, just like pregnancy. The combo of my chemo feasts and being incredibly hydrated gave me a five-months-pregnant belly. My Cancer Baby.

I even hung out with my stay-at-home mama and maternity leave friends—just like when we were on maternity leave together.

Yet another similarity—hemorrhoids, the ugly truth of both pregnancy and breast cancer treatment!

Then there were the supplements, oh, the supplements. Vitamins for prenatal care, fenugreek for milk production, soy lecithin for plugged ducts. Now, Vitamin D for bone health and to protect against cancer (although, too little too late!), probiotics for gut health, and Vitamins B6, B12, and L-Glutamine powder to keep away neuropathy. Pregnancy and cancer filled my pillboxes to the brim.

While pregnant, I went on runs to keep my body in shape for childbirth, and while in chemo, to stay healthy. I felt like Superwoman for doing any minor exercise—a one-block walk two days after giving birth, a jog two days after chemo. But, as I jogged during chemo, when I saw other women running mid-day, I wondered if they were off work because of cancer, too? I did a quick boob scan and looked for a port—was that short haircut not *just* a fashionable, pixie cut? I thought everyone was a ticking cancer time bomb.

My hair fell out with both a baby and cancer. In pregnancy, a few weeks after giving birth, I lost the extra hair that was not falling out while I was pregnant. In cancer, I lost it after a couple chemotherapy infusions, but then, it was ALL my hair, even my eyebrows and eyelashes. At least I didn't have to clean hair out of the shower drain for months! I did not have to take hair products with me when I swam or traveled, and I could shower any time of the day without worrying about going to sleep or out in the cold with wet hair.

I dug out my nursing bras to use during cancer treatment. Recovering from my lumpectomy, I could no longer wear my supportive underwire bras, but the soft-cotton nursing bras stretched perfectly for my swollen, recovering breast. During chemotherapy, the bras unhooked to give the nurse better access to my port, and during radiation, they were all my burning skin could handle.

Think the pregnancy or infant and toddler years destroy your sleep? Definitely. And so does cancer! As a pregnant person, always having to go to the bathroom mid-night. As a new mom, the baby nursing. Then, when the baby slept for long stretches, staring at the monitor in the middle of the night to make out the rise and fall of his chest, and maybe even sneaking into his room—at the risk of actually waking him—to make sure he was breathing. With cancer, anxiety kept me awake—how did this happen, how long had the cancer been there, where did it spread, was I making the right treatment decisions? Then, even after these thoughts receded and sleep should have come, the treatment steroids kept me awake in the middle of the night.

And, the forgetfulness. As a new mama, I felt like a shell of my former self, not as smart, efficient or social as I used to be. Same with cancer. I forgot things and felt foggy. Chemo brain is a real thing!

There were some perks. I could go swimming during "senior and special needs" hour at the city pools! Pregnancy counted, and so did cancer. When I returned to senior/special needs swimming time during cancer treatment, I saw the same ladies (they did not recognize me, of course, with my bare head and smaller belly) that

I saw three years ago, when pregnant. I cried throughout that first swim.

And, this was another way in which having a baby was just like having cancer: the smallest things made me cry. Walking to pick up food without my baby for the first time. Another senior/special needs swimmer telling me I was an excellent swimmer. The tiniest kindnesses drew a well of emotions. My nerves were so frazzled, emotions so fragile, and hormones completely out-of-whack.

Like having a newborn, my friends set up a meal train and brought me dinner during treatment. People sent texts or emails and did not expect me to respond. Even strangers were so very nice: I am fairly sure a police officer did not give me a ticket when he saw my bald, clearly-in-medical-treatment head.

Both cancer and childbirth were really liberating. In childbirth, with no pain killers, I trusted and followed my body. I did not care what people saw or who came and went—and I gave birth at UCSF, a teaching hospital, so a *lot* of people came and went. Afterward, I asked my husband, with a sense of pride and ferocity, "Do you think they heard me down the hall?" His response: "I'm pretty sure they heard you down the street." With cancer, I experienced a similar feeling of liberation, although not because I trusted my body, but because I have cancer! So who gives a fuck?! Walking around the house naked on a rare 85° day, my husband said, "Hey, the neighbors are in their yard and might

94

be able to see you!" My answer: "Who gives a fuck? I have cancer!" Going out bald in the world—same thing.

My husband showed how amazing and supportive he is with childbirth, calming me at critical junctures, understanding me and my freak-outs, and advocating for me with the doctors. And, as I panicked at each chemo—*shit, is this thing really working?*—he listened and soothed my nerves. He was an equal partner in childrearing, and after my diagnosis, he was much more than that. He got our boy ready for school every day, did so much of the bedtime routine, let my piles and messes slide, and has washed all the dishes since my diagnosis.

Both with having a child and having cancer, there were friends who ended up being such a support, unexpectedly, and those who drifted into the shadows. The neighbor who brought a healthy, home-cooked meal—and sometimes even wine—every week. *Every week.* The family and friends who set up a meal train, who got me a wig, who sent cards or care packages or funny distractions, who dug up an old video of my baby saying, "Maman's gorgeous," just as I began losing my hair. Some of them were my oldest friends, but many of them were not. And some of my oldest friends didn't call or check in.

Through pregnancy and having a child, I met so many delightful mamas who have made my life richer. Similarly, one of the wonderful things about having cancer (I cannot believe I used "wonderful" and "cancer" in the same sentence, but it *is* true!)

is the amazing people it has added to my life. The friends and family with whom I have drawn closer. The other survivors, who are open, honest, and raw, and who showed me this can happen to *anyone*. They reassured me that I did not cause this cancer—it was not what I ate, how much I drank, the products I used, the impatience I showed with my mother, or that my life was going too well. They taught me that bad things sometimes happen to good people. They understand me in a way no one else does, because of our shared experience. And they reassure me that, like in pregnancy, hemorrhoids are normal.

With chemo and surgery now in my rearview, I have some space to breathe and reflect. Recently, while at a cancer retreat, I did a labyrinth walk. It reminded me of the labyrinth I walked, while pregnant, at San Francisco's Grace Cathedral. A midwife led us, and, as we walked, we thought about all the strong women who had come before us. When I did the cancer labyrinth walk, I thought of all the women who had faced breast cancer before me, their strength and grace. Like them, I will emerge from the labyrinth, and I will hopefully come out of it braver, stronger, more present.

My Cancer Baby has opened another world to me—one that is scary, painful, and frustrating, but also rich and rewarding. It makes me view and appreciate the world in a way I never had before. Just like having a baby did.

Nine Months and Counting

Julie Morgan

You are nine months old! You have my eyes, anyone can see that. It terrifies me when I think you might have my breast cancer risk, too. I don't (I won't!) live in a constant state of active fear for you, your health, your planet, but, I worry on the regular. I get reminded of the chemical soup into which you were born. The toxins that coursed through my body into yours and now in the air you breathe, food you eat, toys with which you play, and I think, "What have I done, what have we all done?" Babies' little bodies polluted before they take their first breath?! I didn't need to have a baby to make me an environmentalist, a safe chemical advocate, or an activist. But, knowing I am responsible for your little body entering this world does certainly amp-up my sense of urgency.

Four years ago, during cancer treatment, I spent five days in the hospital with a neutropenic fever. After a few months of chemo, my immune system was in the toilet and a simple virus sent me to the ER with a wicked-high temperature. A well-meaning nurse came in to hang my medication. Attempting to make small talk, she asked, "Do you have children?" Upon hearing I did not, she responded, "That's probably better." Better for whom? For what? Better I don't have to care for children while caring for myself? Better no child has to see me in the hospital? Better I never had children? I knew she had no idea how her simple phrase could send a young(ish) cancer patient's mind into a swirl. I have said more than my share of awkward things in my own long nursing career. Such a physically demanding job that requires sharp mental skills does sometimes leave a me at a loss for words, or at least the right ones. Part of me agreed with her.

We didn't plan for you. My forty-year-old post-chemo body didn't miss the one chance it was given that month. I could not help but think, maybe, "this was meant to be" when I found out I was pregnant. Not that I believe that everything happens for a reason. Some may find solace in that phrase, but it can ignite anger in others, when the "everything" that is happening has zero silver lining. This was one of those times when it gave me tingles to pretend it was true and to be so thankful.

You are fun, feisty, loving, and adorable (yes, I do have nice eyes!). While waiting for prenatal testing, I joked that my weak eggs got decimated during chemo and only the healthy ones survived. You are healthy and so strong. You are full of life and potential. I will not, cannot, leave you with this polluted world. I make your dad promise if I die young, he'll make you eat vegetables (of course he knows they need to be organic). There is so much more that I need to teach you and share with you. There are so many things I need to help change in the world. I hope I have the time, as I know far too many women who have not gotten to see their children grow up.

Shit Happens (Or It Doesn't)! And Other Life Lessons: A Letter to My Daughter

Yamini Kesavan Ranchod

To my darling baby girl:

This morning, your eight-month birthday, started out like many others. You were wide awake, a mischievous twinkle in your eye, smiling with your two bottom teeth poking out half-way, and ready to tackle the world. I was struggling to lift my head from the pillow. This is how most of our days begin—a juxtaposition of your boundless energy and infectious smile and my fatigued body and mind, reminding me of a distant time when I last felt that alive and young, of a time when I didn't wake up wondering if I could make it to the end of the day without keeling over in exhaustion, and, if today would be the first day in five-and-a-half years that I didn't feel pain. You may see me as a grown up, but I feel much like you, my darling, like a new babe who needs to close my eyes more than once a day, like a child that becomes cranky and over-tired with too much activity or too many late nights. Today, like every day, I marvel at your sheer zest for life and wonder if I am being the best mother I can for you. I often think that you deserve the "me" from six years ago, but you get the "me" now. What's the difference, you may wonder? I'll get to that.

As our morning routine continues, you sit in your bouncer outside the bathroom door while I take care of my favorite morning business. Ok, let's just call it what it is—my morning shit. And man, do I like a good morning shit. I prefer not to have company for it, but if I had to have anyone, you're not a bad spectator. Depending on how long I'm sitting there, we can get through a few rounds of peek and boo, and several renditions of "Head and Shoulders, Knees and Toes," "Twinkle Twinkle," "The ABCs," "Wheels on the Bus," and "Old MacDonald." My favorite, though, is, "If You're Happy and You Know It." Why? Because when I'm on the pot, and the goods are flowing, I am damn happy and I know it. And, I'm ready to clap my hands and stomp my feet to show it.

Lesson #1: You don't know how much you appreciate smooth plumbing until you've experienced clogged pipes or runny drains (while this may be metaphor for life, darling, I do mean this literally!). And while you may think this the first time in my adult life that I've performed a song and dance routine with another person while I'm on the pot, you'd be wrong. This ain't my first rodeo, baby girl.

Let's rewind. Five-and-a-half years ago, when I was just thirty-one years old, I received a phone call from a radiologist who needed some serious training on how to break bad news to a patient.

Lesson #2: There are a lot of very smart people who never got the memo on compassion or communication. You will want to punch them in the face, but you won't, mainly because it's better to not be arrested for assault.

The news this doctor so poorly delivered: I had breast cancer. What? No. Not now. I was just getting into my life-groove. After years of watching friends settle into their marriages and careers, and a couple of painful setbacks in my life (don't fish, sweet pea, those are stories for another day), I had just met the most amazing man (I'll spare you the suspense: it was your papa) and was half way through finishing my PhD. We had plans to move to California and start a life together. Instead, he moved out West alone, and I moved in with your grandparents to start a year-long treatment protocol. We made things work long distance until I was well enough to join him. Some long distance couples keep the flame alive by sexting, but I sent him awkward chemo selfies— "Hey look at me smiling cheerfully while I'm hooked up to this poison! Thumbs up, winky face!" But, he stood by me, your papa. He is one incredible man.

Lesson #3: there is a partner out there for you who will take your breath away, make you feel beautiful even when you are at your worst, and weather the storms with you. Don't settle for anything less.

When your papa would visit me at your grandparents' house for the weekend, I had conned your conservative grandma into letting him sleep in the same room with me. How? I played the cancer card. Yes, there is a card for that. How can you say no to the girl who has cancer? You can't. The irony was that I was bald, bloated, nauseated, hot flashing and bone-tired. So no "hanky panky." Little did I know that no hanky panky would be an ongoing theme for my life. Cancer treatment has a way of making my third decade of life feel more like my sixth. If I had known I would be spending most nights alternately throwing off the covers as I burned up, and violently pulling them back on as I froze in my own drenching sweat only three minutes later, I probably would have suggested he sleep in the guest room!

Lesson #4: Things don't always work out the way you plan or expect. You may think you're playing your cards right for passion and warm snuggles, but the universe may decide that hot flash/freeze out is a better game for you.

Hot flashes may sound unpleasant, but there is something much more so, which I had the displeasure of experiencing for the first time just after my first chemo. After a couple of days spent trying desperately to poop, I was miserable and in pain. Almost as bad as the constipation was listening to just one more well-meaning person rattle off the perfect solution to constipation. "Hey, did you try smooth move tea?" Yes, and nothing is moving, smoothly or otherwise. "My grandma's boyfriend swears by these stool softeners." Thanks, I've been taking those for days and now I feel worse because your grandma's boyfriend and I have something in common. Finally, I decided I would just sit on the pot for as long as it took and will it to happen. I had been sitting on the pot long enough, crying and moaning, that your grandma was worried and knocked on the door. "Are you ok? I'm coming in." She walked in, closed the door behind her, and looked intently at me. Hmmm. Now what, mom? Are you going stare down my poop until it comes out of its hiding? And, just when I thought it couldn't get weirder, she started singing, to the tune of "Frère Jacques," "Poop is coming, poop is coming, Yami's going poop. Yami's going poop." I would never hear that lovely children's lullaby the same way ever again. "Poop is coming right now, poop is coming right now, yeah, yeah, YEAH! Yeah, yeah, YEAH!"

For just a moment, I forgot my pain. Had the stress of dealing with my diagnosis and treatment finally pushed your grandma over the edge? No, she was just a believer in putting your intentions out to the universe. And, what better way of convincing the universe to send the poop vibes my way than to sing it my very own shit lullaby! So, instead of doing the sane thing and asking her to kindly exit, I began to rub my tummy and joined in, "Poop is coming, poop is coming..." You may be thinking that this is completely ridiculous, my mom and grandma have lost it. But, three minutes and several versus later, I pooped. I'm not exaggerating when I say that it was one of the happiest moments of my life. I got this! I can deal with any shit!

My newly-found confidence in dealing with my shit was deflated a few days later when the side effects switched from constipation to diarrhea. In case you're wondering, I may have been able to sing my shit out, but there isn't a song in the world that can keep that shit in.

Lesson #5: Shit happens. Or it doesn't. You can't predict when or why or how much.

I realize now that I have changed because of the shit that's happened in my life, but I'm no less than I was. I may feel older and exhausted as I try to weather the side effects of ongoing treatment for many more years, but I am stronger, braver, and more prepared to deal with any shit that happens. Most importantly, I am alive—here to shit another day and sing through it all with YOU, my greatest gift.

Although I wish for you a blessed life, my darling, I can't promise you that it will always be giggles and rainbows. It won't. The best I can do is promise that if you face your shit head on, with confidence, you will be ok. And it never hurts to make up a song about it.

All my love,
Mommy

If I Don't

Emily Kaplan

if I don't say it
if I act well and smile
and persevere with strength

and then I get angry
and then you get angry
because I've collapsed

it doesn't have to make sense
it doesn't have to be put into words
allow me my paralysis for now

with your kind
understanding
patience
presence
proximity

I am here always and will heal again

Public Assaults of Preciousness

Angela Raffin

The first time it happened, I was at my first-born daughter's bat mitzvah. It was December 2014, I was newly diagnosed, and nobody around me knew about it. I was hijacked by a Public Assault of Preciousness, or PAP, as I like to call them.

Now, it's happening again at my second-born's band concert. My view softens, and there is movie-like glow to an otherwise ordinary moment. The scene feels so over-the-top "precious" that I begin to tear up. The first few tears I wipe away without notice. I force my thoughts to kitties, puppies, anything other than "this is a moment I am lucky to have." Shit. Panda bears. Sloths. Anything. Nope, the tears are welling up, threatening a full-on, very public deluge if I can't pull it together.

Of course, I don't have tissues because here I am, just trying to live my life like all the other moms—worrying about the summer sandals that my daughter is wearing on this chilly February night because *band members must wear black shoes* and her dressy ones don't fit anymore. My nose is starting to run, and my husband doesn't seem to notice I'm losing it. That old adage, "Don't let worry rob you of your present," runs through my mind, but I'm not capable of rational thought right now. I excuse myself from the squeaky bleachers, mid-song, to walk outside and weep alone.

Two mastectomies, chemo, radiation, an oophorectomy and one of two reconstruction phases are in my 2015 rearview mirror. Despite my insistence on putting it in my *children's* past, it is still in *my* present. I'm apparently doomed to cry at every happy moment with my kids. I don't want them to know that cancer is still a worry, so I smile a little too wide sometimes. When my health is questioned in front of my daughters, I quickly reply, "I'm GREAT!!!" Yes, with three exclamation marks in my voice. I work hard to keep these assaultive, public tears at bay.

My other technique to address the Public Assault of Preciousness: LIE. Look them straight in the eye, and lie through my teeth. A few months ago, I was helping supervise a Girl Scout overnight trip to the lovely Montara Lighthouse. The whales were visible from the shore and putting on a show while I was schlepping sleeping bags and rogue socks back to the car (there is nothing better, or worse, than an overnight with ten-year-old girls). The leader recounted to me that while I was gone, my own little Girl Scout watched the whales breach and said, "Oh, I wish my mom were here to see this!"

Just like that—*Snap!* Breast cancer had me in its clutches again. My throat caught, and I was held captive to the preciousness of being there with my daughter, and, of course, the terror that some day she will have moments without me. This was an ugly cry, the kind where women rub your arm, pat your back and give you their sunglasses to hide the wreckage. I hid on a bench and forced my thoughts to things less desperate and precious.

My daughter rounded the corner, hair whipping in the wind, and as she caught sight of me, her face fell. She walked over and sat. "What's wrong, mom?" I smiled with all my teeth and said, "The whales just make me so HAPPY! Aren't they incredible? I'm just overwhelmed!" This seemed to reassure her, or perhaps she just decided to go along with it.

I'm too young for breast cancer and they're too young to have their lives framed in desperate preciousness, but this is our life right now. In the meantime, my battles with the Public Assaults of Preciousness stand testament to the mundane and sacred that sit side-by-side in our family life.

Now, excuse me while I cry through a soccer game.

New Nipples?

Jen Brand

I was dreading the moment when my four-year-old daughter Talia would notice my new breasts. How would she react? What would I say? Visions of her running out of the room, screaming, passed through my head. I was recovering from a double mastectomy, thanks to breast cancer. This was the first phase in my reconstruction—I had tissue expanders just beneath my skin to make room for implants down the road. I was still getting used to myself in the mirror but was not certain I was ready to go prime time and show anyone else, especially my four-year-old daughter, my new look.

Then, one day, we were on the front steps of our house, working on an art project, and I said I was going to take a shower.

About fifteen minutes later, Talia came into the bathroom to hang out—like only a four-year-old will do. She stood on the other side of the glass shower door, where only steam and water hid my body. I started to panic. I thought to myself, "Shit! It's too soon. The incisions still look too gruesome. What am I going to say?" She asked me to wipe away the steam and water so she could see me. Slyly, I wiped away the area at my eyes. Immediately she said, "No mommy, I want to see your body!" Damn, now what?

With my heart pounding, I revealed my body. She looked me up and down and said, "Um…Mommy, um, where are your nipples?" She asked like it was the most normal question in the world. I responded, "In the operation, the doctors had to remove my nipples because of the breast cancer, but don't worry, I'm gonna get new ones soon." She gave me the oddest look. Then replied, "New nipples? What the heck!"

I got out of the shower and began to dry off. I kneeled down on the ground and let her inspect my body. She pointed to each little wound and asked if it hurt, and each time, I answered honestly. And then, just like that, she ran out of the room, back to her art project. As only a four-year-old will do.

100% a Mom

Lori Wallace

I was first diagnosed with Stage IIA breast cancer in April, 2011. My younger son, Braden, was four-years old, almost five. I started out scared, but optimistic. Like most Americans, I had been brainwashed, by pink ribbon fundraisers, to think that breast cancer was almost cured. Terrified, despite the brainwashing, I took the fighter stance, "It's going to be hard, but I've got this!" Then, a young mother in my cancer community died of cancer. I was dazed, confused. What happened?! Why did she die, when she was trying so hard to live?! What happened to breast cancer becoming a chronic, not terminal, disease?! Then, more young women died. Some mothers, some not, but all strong, wonderful women who did everything that they could to stay alive. It felt like people were dropping like flies. I remember being consumed by anxiety and fear, totally overwhelmed, and crushed by the idea that I could die and my baby wouldn't remember me. Just writing that sentence makes me cry, now, even though he's ten-years old.

I HAVE progressed to Stage IV. I have metastatic breast cancer, but Braden WILL remember me. I have had five years, since initial diagnosis, to create memories with him and try my best to brainwash him to think like me (or at least share my world view!). I will die of this disease, but there's no telling when. Maybe six months, maybe six years. Meanwhile, I LIVE. Every day, I get up and enjoy coffee sitting next to this bigger kid, talking about whatever is interesting that morning.

When I discovered that my disease was, indeed, terminal, I was desperate to DO THINGS. I needed a Bucket List! Bucket Lists are a common topic in Cancerland. Fellow residents post amazing pictures of things on their Bucket Lists—exotic vacations and daredevil activities that make them feel ALIVE, when death is staring them in the face. I needed to create my own Bucket List, but how? I've never had one. It wasn't anything I had ever considered. Making a LIST of things I wanted to do? If I want to do something, I do it...or don't, if I can't afford it. There was no list. So, I tried to think of places I would like to go. I spent months, off and on, watching travel guru Rick Steves and thinking about where, when and how. The more I learned, the more I realized that epic travel requires a lot of planning and is VERY expensive. I want to do something epic, but without leaving my family in debt. I tried recruiting my grown son, Evan, thinking that he could plan a blockbuster adventure for the two of us, but, he wasn't really interested.

As treatment side effects accumulated, and my stamina ebbed, I decided I was going about it all wrong. I was stressing myself out about something that was supposed to be joyful. That's stupid. I needed to switch my focus to easier-on-the-body travel, local and regional. We could tour the American West and spend time on the Pacific Coast. Silly me, people from all over the world travel here. I live within driving distance of several "destinations." We'll just drive and see where we end up!

Then, a few weeks ago, I said something to Braden about puberty, and that it will start changing his body soon. It had come up before, and he pretty much ignored me. THIS time, he had questions. HOW was his body going to change? Why would he feel weird about it, when all his classmates would be going through the same changes? That doesn't make sense. Why did our bodies change this way, and, how DO babies get into a mom's tummy?

This was a Big Deal, for me. I desperately wanted to be the one to introduce the topic to him, but only when he was ready, in a healthy, non-judgmental, respect-and-love-your-body-and-the-bodies-of-others sort of way. Even though I've progressed to Stage IV, and death is sitting here, next to me…waiting, I am still here. I am still here! Most parents dread talking to their kids about sex, but not me. I'd been hoping for it. THIS was huge! This was something worthy of my Bucket List! For me, it's SO much more important than traveling to glamorous locales. What a revelation!

Some days and weeks are better, or worse, than others. Treatment kicks my ass. Braden has seen me puke for days on end and become less "wide" (He notices how wide people are, not fat, which I think is hilarious.). He has been in the infusion room with me, which is generally frowned upon by the doctors and nurses. He has gone to many blood draws with me. He knows my cancer will kill me, but he also knows it could be many years from now. And no matter what happens, he knows that I love him like crazy. Same with Evan. They will always know that I did everything humanly possible to stay here to be their mom. That's another BIG DEAL for me, even more epic than the sex talk.

My message to early stage moms, who are gripped by fear that their babies won't remember them, is this: About 75% of women diagnosed with early stage breast cancer do not progress to Stage IV after "finishing" treatment. For those of us who do, it can take awhile to die. And all that "while" is time to LIVE. Living with a terminal illness is an outrageous, emotional, rollercoaster ride, but, at the beginning and end of each day, IT IS LIVING.

I still hike when I can, and it feels awesome! I volunteer at Braden's school more than many healthy moms. I have spent this entire summer doing fun things with him. We've shared days at the beach, with and without friends, gone to Alcatraz, the San Francisco Museum of Modern Art, camping, and Lake Tahoe. I also focus on the everyday things—I drag him around on boring shopping trips and teach him to eat dinner, without electronic devices distracting him from the meal and conversation. I am 100% a mom and am always here to snuggle and discuss life, even though there are weeks I don't have the stamina to do dishes.

I understand, and remember, that initial fear of both diagnosis and progression. The emotional paralysis. It never completely goes away, but it changes, it softens, at least most of the time. I have learned to give myself room to feel however I feel and encourage the same in everyone else. Feelings are not a weakness. They are what make us human. Even sadness and grief. I may not feel like it, right now, but I'll be ok, and my kids will be ok, too. That is the #1 item on my Bucket List. That, no matter what happens, we will ALL be ok.

On Being A Deedahdah

Doreenda Ziba

When my nephew tells me over the phone, in half English and half Farsi, "Deedahdah Deedahdah, beeyah our khooneh," or, "Come to our house," it nearly breaks my heart. It makes me sad that I'm far away, and that I can't, as he demands, come to his house. And, it simultaneously makes me so happy that he wants to see me and have me around.

I remember after my mastectomy, the nurse started asking me questions about my age and type of cancer. When I told her I was thirty-five, she replied the usual, "Oh, too young!" Then, she asked the dreaded question, the question I knew was coming: "Do you have kids?" I immediately knew what she was getting at, and responded, wearily, "No." She breathed a sigh of relief, and I knew what that sigh meant. I'd heard the spiel before, in different ways, with different tones of voices, but, it's essentially: "Good thing you don't have kids because that means if you die, it's ok, since nobody REALLY needs you."

I got angry. I was on a ton of morphine, just having gotten out of major surgery and dealt a completely new body that I couldn't even feel at that point. I asked her, in a saccharin-sweet voice, "Do you have kids?" I suspected she didn't. She said, "No, I don't, but my sister has kids. Does yours?"

I said no, not yet. And I thought to myself, "Your sister having kids doesn't count. You only get to take credit if you have to birth them, pay for them and lose sleep because of them."

Then, I fell into a morphine-induced sleep.

But, I never forgot that conversation.

My hypothetical child had been on my mind since the moment I was diagnosed. I remember thinking, right after the fateful phone call, that I made a grave mistake by not having a child yet. I was thirty-five. I had no excuse. And there I was, single, childless, motherless, too, completely at a loss as to who exactly would take care of me through chemo. My mother had me, my sister Amanda, and my dad to care for her during her illness. I had no kids and no husband, and thought for sure I would not be able to survive chemo without that type of support network.

More importantly, I felt, at that moment, that my life was meaningless. I was going to die without leaving any footprint, without achieving anything great, without passing on the utter awesomeness of my parents—and I felt guilty for not doing that. I felt like I squandered the intensity and the love that my mother gave me, and the kindness and compassion of my father.

And, I took these things from them and used them all on myself without giving my parents the satisfaction of passing the love and compassion and intensity on to the next generation. What a spoiled brat I was.

So, when this nurse came to me after my surgery, she was pouring salt onto the wound.

Fast forward a few years. Amanda gave birth to a little-over-nine-pounds of sweet perfection. Eitan became the apple of my eye. And my father's eye, and my sister and my brother-in-law's eyes.

Before Eitan was born, my Reiki practitioner, Michelle, told me that babies are healing. I had already decided that I would try to stave off going back to work after cancer treatments until Amanda did, post-birth, so I could concentrate on my yoga certification and bonding with the new baby. But, when my Reiki practitioner said that, I thought to myself, "Yeah, I could use some healing."

As it turns out, Michelle was right. Babies ARE healing. I cuddled and kissed that baby boy so much. And yet, it was never enough. I could never get my fill of this kid.

It's ironic, though, that from diagnosis until Eitan was born, I thought to myself that by me not having a child, I was being selfish because I wasn't giving enough to my family and the world. When Eitan was born, I realized how much *he* was giving *me*. He truly was healing me.

Sometimes, I think back on that nurse and wonder if her only true crime was that she loved her nieces and nephews and felt just as invested in them as I do in my sister's child and her child-to-be. And, perhaps, that is enough.

Itching for a New Relationship

J. Mork

Cancer:

I am breaking up with you.

I admit,

you ravish me,

even though you mostly make me tired, grumpy and bitter. That is

never sexy. You want expensive treatment which I cannot afford,

never respecting my boundaries financially or emotionally.

You are unreliable, never saying when you will show up again.

All of my friends do NOT like you.

You are a thief of time.

We never had that "couple look."

You dictated that I would never have children.

I am so over you.

Please, I just want to move on and see others.

Actually, Eczema and I are dating now, and he is no flake.

Good-bye, Good-luck, Bonne Chance,

J. Mork

P.S. I will be at the Breast MRI Center at 7:45-9:00am Thursday, so please don't show up unexpectedly.

You are not welcome.

A Love Letter to Paolo Porto

Kristen Zeitzer

Dear Paolo,

We met under unusual and difficult circumstances. I was a week away from starting chemo, looking for love wherever I could find it.

The interventional radiologist set us up on a blind date on July 30, 2014. My friend who escorted me to the meet up liked the name Paolo Porto and the idea of me acquiring an Italian boyfriend. At least sixteen future dates were already scheduled, so doesn't that qualify for referring to you as my "boyfriend?"

Our first meeting lasted hours longer than expected. Silly me for thinking we would have a simple coffee chat in the surgery and treatment rooms; instead, we had to wait in line while others talked and prepped.

For days after, I couldn't stop thinking about you. Your placement just under my right clavicle made moving anything excruciatingly painful. The nurse couldn't even find you for my initial chemo, our first non-blind date. I took jabs to the left and below; you continued to play hide and seek for half an hour. Not the time to be playing games, Paolo!

123

I believed our relationship would continue down this adversarial path. After all, most of my long-term relationships were like this. What am I doing, I thought, partnering with another man who was out for himself without regard to how I feel?

However, you proved me wrong. Once the swelling from our blind date went down, the nurses could easily find your little bumpy triangle.

Through chemo, blood draws, and heparin flushes that left a bitter, chemical taste in my mouth, I depended on you. You delivered what I needed, and took what I had to give. You never gave me an infection, and you supported me through all of my breast cancer treatments.

When chemo ended, my oncologist told me to break up with you. But, I wasn't ready for our relationship to end. We needed to stay together longer. Perhaps just until my one-year Cancerversary, when I would have my first post-treatment PET scan.

We checked in to the nuclear medicine department together, and I was grateful you were there with me. But, they didn't know how to use you! I fought for your right to participate, as we were a couple, bound together. They eventually found a nurse who could help, who knew how to handle you. And we made it through together—no evidence of disease!

Sometimes relationships, however successful, have to end. It's not you, Paolo, it's me. I'm moving on, past chemo, past active treatment. After a lot of introspection, heart-wrenching conversations with my girlfriends and family, and impulse shopping, I asked my plastic surgeon to remove you during the next phase of reconstruction.

But, not ready for a forever goodbye, Paolo, I'm keeping you in the friend zone.

Now, you rest on my desk, a handsome reminder of our nurturing relationship. Thank you, beautiful Paolo. Ti amo!

Always,
Kristen

Love is in the Mending

Kelsey Crowe

Thank you for touching my hand while sharing your expert opinion. I mean it. Thank you.

I wish I were more central in your life, like your sister. The one you will fight for, harder than anyone else.

Damn that you try to get home by 6pm. That you have a family that depends on you. That I fight with all the charm I can muster to be more than I am to you. To be someone like your sister.

In your house: I am the patient who has been emailing too much. The patient who is irritable about her diagnosis.

In mine: I am the mother, the wife, the daughter, and I might be dying. Am I dying?

You called me past 8pm on your way home. The reception was poor; the effort was imperfect. It was what I needed.

You said you believe me. You said that you are sorry. I am too.

Thank you for laughing. For asking. For taking my hand. For doing everything you can.

Cures are not guaranteed, but there is yearning for love in the mending.

I wish I were your sister.

V. ILLUMINATION

"Don't loaf and invite inspiration; light out after it with a club, and if you don't get it you will nonetheless get something that looks remarkably like it."

— Jack London, "Getting Into Print," in *Practical Authorship*

I'm a Keeper

Sarah Haberfeld de Haaff

Today, I was in the car, wrestling with the absolutely ridiculous sunshade visor thingy for the millionth time, and I just snapped. I gave up. I decided that shit is going in the trash. I hate it EVERY SINGLE TIME I USE IT! It absolutely sucks. No, worse than sucks. What is a phrase for worse than sucks? Whatever. It causes me great and significant aggravation.

You know the kind I am talking about? It's silver on one side, black on the other. You put it in the front window of the car. In order to work, it is wedged under the flip down visors and supposedly keeps the car cooler in the sun. My husband Greg is a big fan of these things and is quite diligent about using them. I never actually used one until I met him. He convinced me they were important.

In his car, he has two individual pieces that fit perfectly under each sun visor and they lay flush with the windshield. Mine, however, is one giant unruly piece that is a little warped and just NEVER cooperates.

NEVER.

It's totally ridiculous and pretty much pisses me off every time I use it. It doesn't really stay evenly under both visors anymore and takes some finesse when putting it up. Unfortunately, that's the easy part. It is the folding it up and putting it away part that drives me to drink. The wires on the outside are *supposed to* twist toward each other and coil in, snapping into a perfect circle that one can "put away."

On the regular, I sit there, sweating, reminding myself to relax, that it's all in the wrists, trying time after time to get it to neatly loop back in on itself, in a perfect little circle. Heck, I'd even settle for a messy oval, if it would allow me to tuck it under the seat.

NEVER HAPPENS!

Many times I get to the fifteenth or sixteenth attempt and give up. I yell profanities at it and throw it into the backseat where it sits, dejected, completely covering my two kiddie car-seats. Obviously this is only my strategy when I am alone and the car-seats are empty. When the kids are with me, I may try a few extra times, while trying to remain calm, but usually end up shoving it into the trunk so we can move on with our lives.

In case I haven't made myself clear… I fucking HATE that thing.

But yet, for some reason, it continues to live in my car. I have kept it around, and it is still the bane of my existence. I never even open it up anymore because it's simply NOT WORTH IT. But, have I done anything about it? Have I made a step toward getting rid of it or buying a new one? NO. It never occurs to me. I have just assumed it was better than nothing.

Today was different though. Today I had a moment. I was getting in my car in the covered and dark oncology parking lot, the sunshade the furthest thing from my mind, and I accidentally bumped into it with my elbow and the ENTIRE FREAKING THING POPPED OPEN, taking up the whole front seat, sitting there staring at me, taunting me.

I snapped, yelling, "I FUCKING HATE YOU!" and opened my door, grabbed the damn thing, walked to the nearest trash can and tried to shove it in.

But, do you think it fit?

NOOOOOO. Of course not, because it's an ASSHOLE.

I drove away, shaking my head, wondering why on earth I had kept it so long in the first place. Why would I keep something around that was so irritating, when I was so over it?

Because I do. I am a keeper. I keep things and people. Especially things, (just ask my garage or my closet), but also some people. I just hang on 'til the bitter end, and then suffer when I have no more room (things), or they disappoint me again and again (people).

I keep my oncologist around when she continues to say stupid, hurtful things. Why? Because she is also incredibly smart and has done some things right, and it's a lot of work to find a new doctor—something I haven't had the time or energy to do. But really, why would I drag my feet ending relationships that aren't working?

Because apparently, I have an open door policy and give everyone the benefit of the doubt. And, most of the time, that works out really well. People are allowed to make mistakes, and I am allowed to make mistakes. The relationship gets better and stronger as a result.

Now, I am not talking about people that give up way too easily, the ones that are like, "If it gets a little inconvenient, I'm so outta here." That's a whole different category. I have an ex-boyfriend in that category and don't worry, he's probably not reading this, because let's face it, cancer is pretty darn inconvenient.

We were friends on Facebook and in person when we would occasionally bump into each other. I assumed he had deactivated his Facebook account when I tried to tag his sister and him in a funny video, a video of a comedian skit from their childhood that we had listened to together many years ago. I thought they would enjoy it too. His name wouldn't show up, so I just tagged his sister. I didn't think much of it until a girlfriend was visiting and mentioned something he recently posted. In order to prove to her he was no longer on Facebook, I typed in his name. See? Nothing, doesn't exist. So then, she got on her account and whoop, there he was.

Ouch. Apparently he IS still on Facebook, and not only unfriended me, but blocked me as well.

Seriously? What are we? Thirteen?

Or forty and married with children?

Can't you just hide me if you don't want to see my posts? I would NEVER unfriend a friend. Never. If you're a regular healthy friend, or a friend with cancer. The latter would be all the more reason to keep you around—I would want to know you were ok or send support if you weren't.

But, that's me, I am a keeper.

And, most of the time, it really does work out. Aside from the sometimes insensitive oncologist and the shitty sunshade/visor thing, I don't have that many other complaints.

WELL, ok, maybe one more thing. This whole cancer thing, too. Perhaps I have been keeping that around for WAY too long. It doesn't serve me anymore. It often irritates me. It gets in the way and frustrates me to varying degrees. I really need to try becoming a "get-ridder-of-er," instead of a keeper. A get-ridder-of-er of cancer. That would be nice.

This weekend, we had some fabulous help clearing out and organizing our garage. We hired some wonderful friends to come out to assist in the process.

It was definitely hard, but, ultimately, felt good. It turns out, I am quite emotionally attached to all of our baby/small kid things and had to breathe through some of that. But, getting rid of old graduate school books and things I haven't looked at in years was awesome and freeing. My dear husband kept giving me high fives when I said, "Get rid of it!" I felt like I was on a weird game show.

I mentioned I was wrestling with the sunshade thing at my oncology appointment. I was there because I haven't been feeling that well lately so did more blood work and met with my oncologist. She is worried that my recent fevers, stomach pain and general malaise could be due to an enlarged liver, which is not good for a person with metastatic cancer. I am really hoping that is not the case, because that would mean the liver metastases are growing.

It's hard to imagine, because everything else has been looking so good. My blood work results are better than ever—my platelets are at 148, right near normal range! As my biochemist said, I am like a normal person.

So how could metastases possibly be growing, when I am, in fact, getting better? The bone metastases have definitely responded to the barrage of things I have thrown at them—they look smaller from scan to scan. We did a CT scan of my liver back in the spring as a baseline, and we planned to do one in late summer to see if it stayed the same, got smaller, or…the not-as-pleasant-option.

I walked out of today's appointment with a CT scan appointment card for 7:30am tomorrow. I made it to my car, barely holding it together, and then proceeded to yell profanities at an inanimate object and attempt to throw it in the trash.

So yeah, it's possible that there may have been a little more to it than just the ridiculous sunshade.

But, it's still an asshole. Good riddance.

Let me just say that a 7:30am appointment has NEVER been a good option for me. My doctor is thirty minutes away, and I am not a morning person. Without kids, it would've been a stretch. But, it's even less of a good idea now. I struggle to get going in the morning on a good day.

My amazing husband has stepped up in ways that I can't even begin to thank him for. The morning routine has fallen mostly on his shoulders AND he does it seamlessly AND still manages to get a workout in. I can't imagine having the energy for exercise AND getting breakfast ready these days. There is a truly remarkable man living with us and his name is Greg, or Daddy, depending on who you ask.

I was still processing the idea that my liver could be causing all of my weird symptoms, so when they handed me the appointment card, I was lost in thought and unable to say, "That does not work for me." See, I even keep appointments that don't work for me! I thought about it a lot on the way home and knew that I would have to change it, but it was only after talking to my mom that I found my resolve.

Because REALLY, 7:30am does not work for me.

I then promptly realized that tomorrow is August 5th, and August 5th DOES NOT WORK FOR ME EITHER.

August 5th is kind of a bad day around here.

August 5th, 2011 was when I got the phone call with the dreaded breast cancer diagnosis. I was at the park with my kids, and the conversation and then swirling trees and spinning ground will be forever stamped in my mind.

August 5th, 2013 was the day I received the phone call from my oncologist in which she told me they found breast cancer cells in my bone marrow, placing me with Stage IV metastatic breast cancer.

So now, here we are, August 5th, 2014, and I simply CANNOT have that scan tomorrow. That would be like a really bad version of *Groundhog Day*. What if it is more bad news?

Maybe I would break the cycle, and it would be positive news. But, I don't know if I am willing to take that chance. Then again, postponing it a day or two could ruin another perfectly decent day in August, if it is actually bad news. And, I used to LOVE August.

See, the keeper in me is pretty hard to squash. It's quite difficult for a keeper to know when to keep and when to throw away.

Turns out, after talking to my mom who knows me really well, it doesn't really matter. The 7:30am thing trumps the August 5th thing anyway.

So, I rescheduled. I am still learning.

Baby steps.

Sarah died from metastatic breast cancer on February 23, 2015 at the age of forty.

The Cancer Odyssey

Kate Holcombe

A year out from diagnosis, I've been feeling much like Odysseus, that humbled hero from the Greek epics, remembering his many long years in battle, and that, after nine years fighting the Trojans, it took him another ten years just to find his way home again.

I am not one for battle analogies and never viewed this as a fight, just a circumstance to overcome and move through as gracefully as possible. And yet, lately, my circumstance has left me feeling unprepared for the effort required, the trials along the way, and the long journey back home.

Journey—such strong distaste I have for that word. Since diagnosis, I've referred to it only as "adventure." "Adventures in Cancerland," I would say. All the tests of mettle, resilience, strength, both inside and out, are just adventures that have appeared before me, opportunities to find my own way through and back home to myself once again.

But oh, what a ride, this one! Feeling tossed about the sea by the angry Poseidon, sometimes within sight of my homeland, only to be blown back into rough waters again, lost and adrift, depending upon the gods, on anyone, for some anchor in this storm. For even Odysseus, were it not for the blessings of the grey-eyed Athena, would still be held captive on Calypso's hidden isle, no doubt, moored to his perch upon the cliff's edge, wind-whipped and weary, gazing out over the waves, pining for his own hearth.

Do I fear the interference of the gods? Certainly, though, I would not have survived without the grace and gifts of many—too many to be named—and am indebted to my own community of most venerable Phaeacian hosts, bestowing food and broth, comfort and shelter, good company, many laughs and much merriment, transportation, and gifts both large and small for the voyage ahead. Even my medical team was part of the kindnesses— my medical oncologist holding my arm, gently massaging scar tissue, post-surgery; my radiation oncologist and her nurse, lovingly tending to my third-degree burns, patiently picking off the black, charred skin, applying salve and clean dressing to the open and oozing sores with such tenderness, it almost brought me to tears. And, above all, those elite few who, like Athena, revealed themselves as goddesses in human form, providing infinite love, endless friendship and care, immeasurable encouragement and guidance, appearing out of nowhere, seemingly always at my side.

And, yet, even with the loving support of so many, still feeling so utterly lost and alone.

So lest you even think it, fools, hear me now and be clear:

cancer is most assuredly NOT a gift, and anyone who claims as such insults those of us who have clung to rafts with salt-stung faces, ravaged by the squall, not sure of our next breath, fearing the siege will surely suck us under into the blackness. For while gifts do present themselves and certainly abound, constant toil and the threat of peril are never far.

The enchantress Circe, goddess of herbs and potions, warned Odysseus of the Sirens, those Sirens! Like the cries of those whose fear was too great, whose ignorance could not be denied, or the selfishness of human beings expressing their own sewage around this dreaded disease, the mire of their own anxiety and powerlessness, all of it threatened to pull me under: "How could YOU get cancer?" "You're the healthiest person I know!" "If YOU can get cancer that means *I* might get cancer!" "What if *I* get cancer?" they'd ask, terror stricken. "Are you going to die?" "You're going to be fine, right?" They frantically searched for some reason, some answer, some way they can feel themselves safe and immune, as if the diagnosis were contagious. Or those whose fear was so great they just disappeared completely.

Which was worse? Those who thoughtlessly blurted out their own selfish interests, or those who vanished?

So, like Odysseus, I kept forging ahead. And, while I heard the Siren voices, I made sure I was bound tightly to the mast, so that I could not be pulled forever from what I know to be true, refusing to take in their song. And, I never took it on: other's reactions, nor the disease itself—it's just a diagnosis, a situation, and a grave one at that, to be thoughtfully and carefully worked through. It is not who I AM. And so, I keep rowing for shore, bracing myself for the next task ahead, even through each "inescapable threat."

My choices in treatment often felt much like navigating through those mythical sea monsters, always, as Homer articulated in *The Odyssey*, the "narrow path between two bad choices" of Scylla and Charybdis: the six-headed sea monster "like nightmares of ferocity," who snatched away so many rowers, or the whirlpool into the abyss that "lurks below to swallow down the dark sea tide." There is no good choice, but choices must be made and consequences dealt with. There is always a sacrifice. There is no use in looking back or grieving for too long those parts of myself that were ripped from the vessel by the fangs of the sea monster as the ship threaded past.

Sometimes, I feel a strength within I have never known, almost invincible. Many days, I feel like a withered old man, creaking and aching, crippled inside and out, from side effects I could have never imagined. So distant from myself, so unlike me, and so, so tired. Everything takes such effort, and yet, like Odysseus, I keep holding on, keep angling for shore.

What is it that keeps me going? How do I hold all these new parts of myself? And what will await me when I finally feel I have arrived back home on my own shores, the steadiness of solid land beneath my feet once more, after so long at sea?

Already, I am so changed in appearance that I have passed unrecognized by many who have known me for years. When Odysseus finally steps onto Ithaca once more, he is so weathered and worn, it is only his faithful and beloved old dog who wags his tail in recognition, contented at his master's return after all these years. Even his own dear Penelope is unsure it is truly her husband returned, after all.

Surely, there are victories to celebrate, losses to mourn, and much to complain about, but there is also joy, newfound strength, lessons learned, and renewed ways of being. And truth be known, I have never had much affinity for complaints, finding them futile and boring (After all, why look for blame or waste energy grumbling? It's better to set my sights on how to find a solution and move forward as positively as I can.). And, while Odysseus had much to complain of himself, the story only reveals his perseverance, tenacity, enduring courage, mighty will, and relentless efforts to find his way home again.

I have always lived fully and wholeheartedly, always appreciating each day, and I truly love my life (No thanks, cancer, I didn't need you to teach me any of that. Remember, NOT a gift!). And, now, I'm living and loving with even more gusto—if I'm hanging onto the wreckage for dear life, at least I try to enjoy it as much as possible. That's what I teach as a yoga and healing practitioner for other cancer patients, right? If I can't change the circumstance, I can at least make the best of it.

So, I turn my face back into the wind, prepared as best as I can be for more swells and adventures, grateful that I don't look in the mirror much or pay attention to scars, for certainly I have changed at every level, as I still search, still long for my own hearth, trusting I will find my way back home once more.

The Talisman

Ami Dodson

The first time I was diagnosed with cancer, I was twenty years old. The swollen lymph nodes on the left side of my neck were Hodgkin's Disease, a type of lymphoma common in young women and very curable. The "common cold cancer," the doctors joked. "You're lucky," they said. I was the only twenty-year-old I knew with cancer; this didn't feel lucky to me.

Curing me took three surgeries, twelve weeks of aggressive radiation therapy that spanned my chin to my belly button, the partial loss of my hair, dropping more weight than was healthy, nausea, vomiting, and skin burns that made people think I'd just returned from some sun-scorched island and forgotten to apply sunscreen. I have scars from the surgeries. For several years afterward, both my feet were tinged a faint blue from the dye they injected between my toes, illuminating the cancer where it was hidden in my body, lit up by the radioactive isotopes like extra bright stars in a cloudy night sky.

But, I was lucky.

Other people were not lucky. At the time, a dear family friend had been battling throat cancer, with limited success. Rick had never smoked a single cigarette his whole life, yet there was the tumor—dogged and persistent. When he visited my father, Rick took me aside and told me what to expect from the radiation: coughing, weight loss, bone aches and phantom pains that would make me think the cancer was punching my insides with tiny fists grown just for the occasion. I was twenty and fearless and didn't really believe him. When I soon learned how right Rick was, I felt again the bitter unfairness of my "lucky" cancer.

Rick had spent much of his career in the import/export business, and that summer he made a final trip to Hong Kong to close out some of his affairs. While he was away, a small package arrived in the mail for me: a card from Rick with a gift inside. The package revealed a delicate gold necklace with a fragile pendant of a Chinese symbol I did not recognize. The card read, "This character means 'long life' in Mandarin. I got one for me, too. May it work for both of us.'"

I was deeply touched by Rick's gesture, but being a pseudo-punk hipster, living in the Pacific Northwest in the mid-1990's, I couldn't possibly wear gold. So, I took the charm to a local tattoo parlor, and much to my father's eternal chagrin, I had the design tattooed on the back of my upper left shoulder in black outline with a scarlet-red fill. I kept the necklace and its charm in my jewelry box, feeling its quiet strength emanating from within.

It wasn't much longer before the throat cancer finally got the best of Rick. I wept bitterly when he died because by then I was better—graduated from college, living a cancer-free life, lucky—and our talisman had not protected him nearly as well.

When Rick died, I was working as a temporary receptionist at the Dana Farber Cancer Institute in Boston. I checked in new patients, showed them where to go for blood draws and made sure they found the right doctor's office within the labyrinthine cancer center. I had been there a month when a new patient arrived, named Joe. He was young—just a few years older than me—and handsome, and even though he didn't look it, very sick. He'd gotten one of the unlucky cancers: melanoma. With the same fearless recklessness of my own youth, he hadn't bothered to have a suspicious mole examined until he was Stage IV. We all knew what that meant.

We would chat amiably when he came in for his increasingly-frequent appointments. I'm sure in his mind I was just a kid—twenty-two, barely out of college, temping in a place I would never be qualified to work. But, in my eyes, he was enough like me that it scared me to know his cancer was not the lucky kind.

I worked at Dana Farber for only a few months; I had decided to move to Connecticut to follow a boy who didn't love me, though I would not realize it for another year. Before leaving, and in flagrant violation of hospital policy, I looked up Joe's home address in Boston. I wrote him a letter about my own cancer experience, and I enclosed the charm that Rick had given me. I told Joe its story, and said that I hoped he would get better soon. I asked him to someday pass the talisman on to someone else, once he didn't need it anymore.

I don't know what happened to Joe after that. I can only assume he died, since I know that Stage IV melanoma is a frightful, vicious disease. I hope he was able to send the charm on to someone else—some other stranger navigating their own cancer experience who may have benefited from its strength, if only for a short time.

Fifteen years later, cancer found me again. Breast cancer, most likely secondary from the radiation to my chest all those years ago. The tattoo on my back has faded over time, and I wonder if I had taken better care of it, if I had touched it up as the red began to bleed into the black, making the whole design softer, blurrier, would it have protected me better? But, I am lucky this time, too: it's virtually certain that after the many surgeries, the chemo, the total hair loss, the breast reconstruction, the sickness and the mess—after all of that has come and passed—I will live again cancer-free for some unknowable length of time.

I've thought of my talisman often over the years, wondering if it's made its way around the country, helping and consoling those who need it. Or, if perhaps it never left Joe's closet and has been relegated to the dusty boxes of memory.

I still hold some hope that I may see that small gold charm again, my original talisman. In these days of hyper-connectivity and social media networks that were nascent dreams during my first illness, I like to think it might be possible that one day I'll receive a small package in the mail.

Who knows?

Apparently, I am lucky.

MRI MacGyver

Natalie Buster

It haunted me. Stalked me. Harassed me. Threatened and abused me. It kept me up at night, heart racing, fingers trembling. It caused me to weep when describing the reality of it to my family.

Yes, the diagnosis of breast cancer at the age of forty was terrible. But, what was more terrifying was the certainty that I would once again be face to face with my nemesis: Big Bad Needle.

For as long as I can remember, I've been deathly afraid of needles. It's always a huge badge of courage for me to get my blood drawn, or even (gasp!) donate blood to a worthwhile cause. It's not that the pain is intense. It's more of a phobia, one that's been ingrained in me, perhaps even embedded in my DNA.

My mother has notoriously small and wily veins, as did her mother before her. When my dear grandmother was going through dialysis, I can remember the mask of pain and fear she wore as the technician prepped her arm, and then the stent in her chest. I've inherited those tiny veins, as well. As a child, I had to have my blood drawn for my first routine physical, only to emerge with dark bruises decorating the insides of my arms. I remember going home afterwards and being treated to a popsicle while watching my favorite show, MacGyver. He never seemed to get bruises.

It was with this awareness of my challenging veins firmly stitched in my memory that I entered the Sisterhood of the MRI.

"I have tricky veins," I warned the technician, who smiled at me and started poking away. First in one arm, then the other. Wrist, back of hand. "Goodness, you're right!" Her image began to swim before me, and I felt a sudden pounding in my ears. I requested a glass of water, and another technician who could maybe, pretty please, try a smaller needle, perhaps one of those exquisite "butterfly needles" that I had heard such great things about.

Hot compresses were applied to the crooks of my elbows. I was given a warmed blanket to stop the shivering. After sixty minutes, we finally got it in! "My troubles are over," I thought. Now I can just lie down and relax in the thrumming MRI machine. In the fog around me, angels adorned in jewel-toned scrubs hovered, cradled, soothed, and murmured quiet encouragement as I kept still. Very still. Oh, so still.

I was wheeled facedown into the MRI for a series of pictures. Contrast, no contrast. There was a consultation, then a numbing shot. After that stinging bee, I felt nothing but the warmth of angels' comforting hands on my back, while the radiologist drilled, scooped, and collected her specimens from my left breast.

Prior to the procedure, the doctor said to me that there's a ten percent chance that the images of the four new spots that were there on the MRI two weeks ago may not be there anymore, and, of course, I was hoping for that, that there would be no reason for a biopsy. But alas, she found them shimmering on the scan.

Despite the news, I was feeling pretty good. Warm, well cared for, loved.

Until the bleeding wouldn't stop.

Apparently, my "tricky veins" were also quite capable of gushing blood.

I had been encouraged to be off any blood thinners like Ibuprofen, and I was religious about that.

The angel assigned to me was so afraid of hurting me after the Insertion of the IV debacle. She kept a cloth against my biopsy site with light pressure. I encouraged her to apply stronger pressure, but she demurred. After forty-five minutes, we thought we had stopped the blood enough to apply the steri-strip bandages to the two biopsy-needle entry points. I was shivering so hard by this point, because the MRI room was glacially cold. Apparently, my veins hadn't received the memo about the frigid temperature and would not constrict and stop bleeding. The angels did their best to keep me covered up, but my body had enough.

The rush of blood started again during the last stop to get a mammogram that documented the indicator clips inside my breast. I was quickly casting the narrative in my head to be That One Time My Breast Would Not Stop Bleeding, a new MacGyver episode. Which actress would play me? Blood streaks decorated the mammogram compression paddles like a ghoulish Rorschach test. I saw faces laughing at me in the blood blots, dancing in front of my unfocused eyes. More pressure, stronger this time. "Can't send you home when you're still bleeding!" Another forty-five minutes later, I emerged with my sports bra padded and an ice pack protruding from my left armpit.

When I showed my husband my battle scars, I saw that the bandages were soaked with fresh blood. He quickly ran to the drug store to get more bandages, which sealed off the area, but quickly filled with blood as well.

Must keep pressing. More pressure. My turn, your turn. So tired.

What would MacGyver do? Didn't he once construct a makeshift tourniquet out of bungee cords? Surely I could save my boob in the same way. I ransacked my closet, found my expensive Italian leather belt, tied it around my chest, cinched it tight, and hoped for the best.

I woke up the next morning to unstained sheets. Little baby scabs had formed on the left side of my left breast. We did it! I rolled onto my right side. MacGyver would be proud.

I'm Looking for the Truth

Meaghan Calcari Campbell

ATM is...

a) A machine that spits out money.

b) A gene that when mutated, increases one's risk of breast cancer by 25-40%.

c) Short for ativan, tequila, and marijuana.

While I'd really like to spend time with a) and c), I am learning more about b).

When I was diagnosed with breast cancer in 2012, I went through genetic testing for the BRCA gene mutation. The geneticist said it would be highly unlikely that I would carry the mutation, given my family history and ethnic makeup. She was right—no mutation.

While waiting for the results to roll in, though, I was snowed in by the "what if" questions. Will I have a double mastectomy? Will we be able to separate out our embryos for those that carry the mutation? Will I ever eliminate my risk of breast cancer?

When the results came back negative for the mutation, I heaved multiple sighs of relief. One less layer of complexity to maneuver. One less arrow in the quiver.

This cancer thing, pssh, a total fluke. A freak incident. Bad luck, like walking right into the path of a lightning bolt. Sure, I asked, "Why me?" And sure, I blamed myself for a litany of things that I did to cause my cancer (e.g., too much cheese, too many veggie corndogs in college, too many parabens in my shampoos, too few babies before I was thirty). But, the universe's randomness brought an iota of comfort. The quote from *Zen and the Art of Motorcycle Maintenance: an Inquiry into Values* rolled around in my head: "For every fact there is an infinity of hypotheses."

So, I moved forward with treatment, procedures, a plan.

Then, this Fall, while cruising around on some oncology science portal—a pretty sexy Friday night if you ask me—I noticed a certain gene mutation that is common is both renal clear cell carcinoma, which my dad has, and breast cancer, which I had. I pounded out a quick note to my oncologist asking for the details. She agreed further testing would be practical and referred me to the geneticist. I had an hour-long appointment, mapping my whole family tree (again), tracing my family history (again), and getting my blood drawn (again). They said, "The chances of there being a smoking gun here are really tiny. Don't expect any clarity."

I mostly forgot about it.

Then, I ordered my husband Mike a 23andMe genetics kit for his birthday gift, thinking, "Cool, maybe we'll both learn something interesting on this gene stuff."

In between scrambling for last-minute Christmas gifts and watching our red wine intake at holiday parties, Mike and I went to the genetics appointment together. We entered the exam room where three doctors, in freshly pressed white coats, sat surrounded by stacks of paper. Not a good sign, even for a teaching hospital.

"Well, we may have found our smoking gun."

Dry mouth, ringing ears, sweaty palms.

The smoking gun is called the ATM mutation. The doctors shared that we all have the ATM gene, but very few of us have the mutation. Only recently, the mutation has been found to correlate with an increased risk of breast cancer in women.

This mutation also has zero relationship to renal cancer, so my initial inquiry for this additional genetic screening didn't pan out in relevance.

Where does that leave me, then?

I went from a relieved, post-treatment breast cancer survivor to an angry and high-risk breast cancer survivor.

I'm angry that I'm catapulted squarely back into Cancerland, and that there doesn't seem to be a way to forever put cancer in the past. I'm angry that no one tested me for this three years ago, likely because of the costs of genetic testing at the time. I'm angry that I might have made different surgical choices then, that maybe I would have had that double mastectomy. I'm angry that my left "healthy" breast falls into a higher risk pool now. I'm angry that I had to ask for this test. I'm angry that I need more frequent and additional screenings from now on, with two MRIs each year, each inducing its own scanxiety. I'm angry that people with the ATM mutation (like me) usually don't receive radiation treatments (like I did), because it increases their risk of getting cancer. I'm angry that I received radiation. I'm angry that the ATM mutation may have contributed to the reconstruction surgical failures and drawn-out recoveries. I'm angry that I spent the last three years thinking my cancer was just a random fluke. I'm angry that I spent three years working through the guilt that I somehow caused my cancer and could have prevented it through lifestyle choices. I'm angry that now my husband has to get tested, because if we both carry the mutation, our embryos and children have a high chance of developing the horrific childhood disease of ataxia. I'm angry that he has to become a patient because of me becoming a patient. I'm angry that my parents might somehow feel implicated, that they have to get tested to inform their own healthcare. I'm angry that I had to bring my family into this conversation, that I have to boil this down to what this means to my brothers and nieces.

In *Zen and the Art of Motorcycle Maintenance*, Robert Pirsig says, "The truth knocks on the door and you say, 'go away, I'm looking for the truth,' and so it goes away." And, the fact of the matter is that even with this genetic mutation, it still might not be the reason or reasons I got cancer. Despite my geneticist's smoking gun reference, we likely will never know the truth, with any certainty.

And, maybe that doesn't really matter anyway.

Science Fiction…Or Non-Fiction

Trinh Vuong

When I was diagnosed with breast cancer in 2011, I quickly lost all sense of vanity. My first thought was survival. Quickly after, my second thought was the new *Transformers* movie is being made, and I am absolutely living to see that. My science fiction-loving heart would not allow anything less!

Because I knew word about my diagnosis would get around quickly between my friends and family, I decided to let people know directly. When I told one of my friends, her first words were, "So, you're going to lose all your hair?!" Since I've been a hairdresser for seventeen years, it's not shocking that this would be everyone's immediate reaction. The irony of a hairless hairdresser. I stuttered, "Uh, yeah. I guess so." I concluded that I would go "Picard," that's Captain Picard for you *Star Trek* fans, at first sign of hair loss. I mean, I have the tools and I know the right people. I prepared my friend that I would call her at initial signs of shedding. My first round of chemo was rapidly approaching.

Chemo, round 1

Day 1

Dear Journal,

Had my first round, and so far, no hair has fallen out, not even shedding normal amounts. Yay, maybe chemo will have a reverse effect on me!

Day 2

Dear Journal,

A cat formed in the tub strainer. Call friend/hairdresser Mimi to bring clippers tomorrow.

Day 3

Dear Journal,

Mentioned to mom that my hair was coming out in clumps. "I should probably sha...ma???" She retreated to the bathroom with sadness. Not today.

Day 4

Dear Journal,

Complained to mom about all the hair on the floor and carpet. To which she responded, "Well, Kim's daughter shaved her hair when it fell out." Here we go. I said, "Oh, yeah? Ok, that's what I'll do." I call Mimi. "Ok, come over. SHE's ready. I mean, I'm ready."

Although I enjoyed the freedom of my "Picard" days, and the ease of throwing on a wig and hat, my hair eventually grew back after chemo ended. And, I survived to see all of the *Transformer* movies.

When my breast cancer returned in 2014, I had to face this challenge all over again. And, thankfully, a new goal for survival was set, with the announcement of production on the *Star Wars films, Episode VII, VIII, and IX.*

Chemo, round two

Day 18

Dear Journal,

Still surprised to be this deep into chemo, and hair is not doing much of anything.

Day 19

Dear Journal,

Starting to shed, but not in big clumps like last time. Boyfriend is in denial about how much is coming out, since I still have a decent amount on my head. He's not ready.

Day 20

Dear Journal,

I AM SO READY to take this shit off. As I gathered hair off my pillow this morning, I said to boyfriend, "This is disgusting. I should just shave this off myself!" He responded with shock, "What??" I cried, "The hair is everywhere! You think you could shave it? Nah. Nevermind. You won't know how to." He quipped, "What? Yes, I can! Where are the clippers? I can do a better job than you!" The challenge was on. Reverse psychology at its finest, but that's our secret.

I am alive to report that I have gotten to nerd-out to *Star Wars Episode VII*, and I look forward to being around to see *VIII* and *XI* in the future.

From the wise words of Yoda in all of this: "Train yourself to let go of everything you fear to lose."

V. NEW NORMAL?

"But what can happen over time is this: You wake up one day and realize that you have put yourself back together completely differently. That you are whole, finally, and strong—but you are now a different shape, a different size. This sort of change—the change that occurs when you sit inside your own pain—it's revolutionary. When you let yourself die, there is suddenly one day: new life. You are Different. New. And no matter how hard you try, you simply cannot fit into your old life anymore. You are like a snake trying to fit into old, dead skin, or a butterfly trying to crawl back into the cocoon, or new wine trying to pour itself back into an old wineskin. This new you is equal parts undeniable and terrifying."

— Glennon Doyle Melton, "I need to tell you something," on *Momastery.com*

A Story in Two Scripts

Kara Carter

A new pharmacist smiles at me.

Picking up please, I give my name.

Tamoxifen for me, Lorazepam for him.

She looks down at the bottles then looks up at me.

Understanding washes over her, pity in her eyes.

My face laughs.

My heart cracks.

Fattening Up

Erin Williams Hyman

What is the antidote to chemo? Hedonism. Pure, unadulterated pleasure-seeking. And, in that, I am finding our move to San Luis Obispo county to be the perfect stomping ground, launch pad, and co-conspirator.

Since the move, I have experienced a profound physical change. The irony was not lost on me that to achieve a new, less stressful and more restorative lifestyle by moving to Morro Bay, I had to pass through one of the most stressful periods of my life— my husband Micah transitioning from a high-profile job, getting a house sold, moving a family of four, uprooting from community, getting the kids through the last of the school year—all while suffering the rigors of treatment for metastatic breast cancer and investigating new experimental protocols. It really can't be any surprise that I would not be able to get through the wash-out period for the trial I wanted to participate in—I was soldiering through, checking down my to-do lists, but the bearing down, resolute, getting-things-done posture is not really the way to get your health back on track. In addition to everything else, I experienced an inadvertent and rapid weight loss. Um, bad sign.

Doctor's prescription: eat cheesecake. First I did a double-take ("Wha...that is NOT what I was expecting you to say!"). But then I didn't need much convincing. Sudden weight loss in cancer patients can be a supremely bad sign: called cachexia, this wasting syndrome robs patients of energy and muscle mass and directly leads to up to one-third of cancer deaths. Eat cheesecake? You got it.

Waking up in our new house in Morro Bay, I can see the ocean. From bed. As soon as the move was complete, I felt physically transformed. Not merely the effect of a new treatment, but also because the burden of stress was gone. No more deadlines, no more traffic jams, no more parking headaches. My body settled and released. Thus commenced the hedonism.

At first, my program of eating to my heart's content was disrupted by one of the first side-effects of the new chemo: mouth sensitivity and taste changes. Couldn't eat anything spicy or crunchy or acidic. Strawberries tasted like metal. Cheese tasted like chalk. Lots of things hurt to eat. So, I started focusing on texture, alternating between healthy delights like avocado-cucumber gazpacho and indulgent treats like Jello Chocolate Pudding—something I hadn't put in my mouth in thirty years, but that satisfied an intense nostalgia. And, I took my son Theo to the supermarket and let him pick out five different ice-cream flavors to store in our freezer.

Around here, there is a farmers' market in one of the

surrounding towns every day of the week. If I miss it, I can still stop in at Dot's farm stand and U-pick on my way home and grab some green beans, corn, or strawberries. Cal Poly has groves of peaches falling off the trees. Our days started to revolve around meal planning: I would begin with huevos rancheros or a really custardy French toast, and by the time I was sopping up the last syrup, I would already be planning the gooey cheese on baguettes and watermelon-feta salad for lunch—or the chocolate mousse I'd need to chill for after-dinner.

After two weeks of probably doubling my calorie intake each day, I saw a nutritionist at Stanford University. I had "only" lost one pound. She told me to start adding avocado, sour cream, nut butters, and coconut oil to everything I could. Still more fat! Well, ok, if you say so.

I have never been a dieter or a calorie counter. I spent way too much time in France to ever go for the nonfat versions of anything. But, I have for sure been dedicated to healthy eating, whole foods, and home cooking for a couple of decades now. And yet, it is surprising to see what it's like to really lift the bar and gorge. You take a step back and see all your prejudices (both good and bad) in a new light.

All of this eating has been accompanied by tons of fresh air and outdoor activity. Luckily, the beauty and the weather here just pull me outside. Our place is located on a State Park, and I walk or hike every day. Yoga, and swimming, too—my energy and endurance have been steadily building.

And now, I can report that I'm back up to my fighting weight. Hooray! But that doesn't mean my renewed food obsession has gone away. My mouth is better now. I can crunch on the mushroom-leek tartines we made last night, and savor the sweetness in the peaches. My mom offered us her ice-cream maker, and, for a second, I hesitated ("another appliance?"), but only for a second. Think of the flavors we'll make with the fruit around here! Raspberries are just around the corner.

They say San Luis Obispo is one of the "happiest" places to live in the U.S. I don't want to overplay this Oprah-endorsed, Tourist-Board-wet-dream sloganeering, but I do have to say that the perfect climate + no commute + natural beauty + food and wine galore + nice people = if not nirvana, is at least rejuvenation. I'm certainly feeling it.

And, if you come to visit, we'll definitely fatten you up. The ice-cream machine is at the ready.

Erin died from metastatic breast cancer on September 18, 2014 at the age of forty-two.

Woman with Cancer in Her Past

Naked Heart

You know where I come from

You know what I've been through

It's not a badge of honor

I work on it constantly

But it's a cross to bear

Striving incessantly for

clear expression of self

While tangled up

In shadows of my past.

Breast Cancer Pink, A Song

Chelsey Hauge and Kate Reid

Lyrics

I think I've got everything under control, it's going to be fine, it's
going to be fine

I'm just trying to find a way to hide this new body of mine

I've got me some of those loose-fitting, with-the-sleeves-rolled-up

Hipster-boyfriend-button-down shirts to pull around my chest

Shirts that make me look like I wouldn't

If you saw me undressed

But there's one more problem, I want to feel normal again, I want
to look normal again

I want to look like what people expect normal should look like

Whatever normal should look like, what does that look like?

I need to fill in this space the surgery left behind

Something to cover up this scar zigzagging across my ribcage and
my mind

Chorus

Cuz they took my left tit away

Like they didn't even give a shit
And I'm on the brink of a fit of rage
Cuz all I'm surrounded with is
Breast cancer pink

At the lingerie store it's all about the perfect rack from that straight
male fantasy
Whether it's Victoria's Secret, or the store for women like me with
partial mastectomies
But excuse me, what's so perfect about
Bras for chicks with no left tit, trying to make me look all
flawless
This is one more space in which my body just doesn't fit

Chorus
Cuz they took my left tit away
Like they didn't even give a shit
And I'm on the brink of a fit of rage
Cuz all I'm surrounded with is
Breast cancer pink

Everywhere I turn all I see is this ghastly pastel shade
Pink bows, pink lace, pink ribbons, pink panties all over the place
What's any self-respecting, no-left-breasted, post-structural
feminist supposed to think?

What can I say?

This gendered cancer game feels like a straitjacket to me

Bridge

And they call us all warriors, as if we're fighting a war

Then they call us badass survivors when we don't die

Well, warriors don't wear pink lace lingerie

And survivors don't hide behind little bows

So gimme some underwear with attitude

Gimme some red and black gitch

Stitch it up with rhinestones and spikes

But nothing proper and nothing lady-like, no!

Chorus

Cuz they took my left tit away

Like they didn't even give a shit

And I'm on the brink of a fit of rage

Cuz all I'm surrounded with is

Breast cancer pink

Free Song Download at www.katereid.net/new_singles1/ and

Music Video at www.chelseyhauge.com/breast-cancer-pink.html

Betty Back-To-Life

Wendy Donner

It ain't over till it's over...actually, still not even then. Betty Back-to-Life shows us just how absurd things can be after cancer treatment, with fallout and side effects from peach-fuzz head to tingling toe.

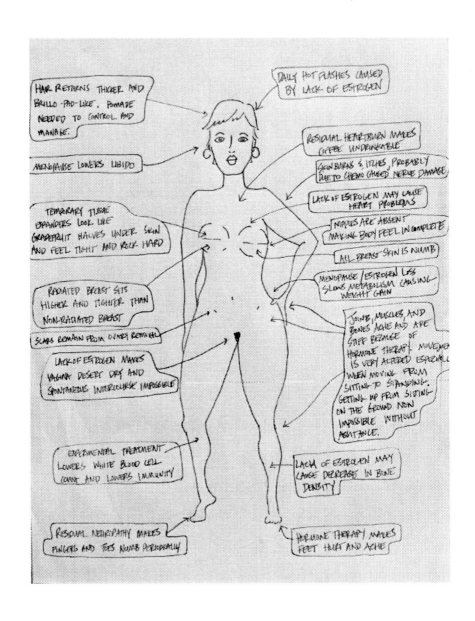

My Mommy Got a Water Arm

Alexandra Fraser

"How do you spell 'cancer,' mommy?" inquired my three-year-old son, Stanley. I asked him if he even knows what cancer is, and he says he doesn't. But, a week later, the two of us were eating ice cream in a fancy waterfront restaurant when Stanley abruptly burst into tears. Sobbing, he said, "I afraid you going to die, Mommy." I held him in my lap at the table, and we wept together until our waiter, looking alarmed, brought the check.

Stanley shouldn't know what cancer is. Sure, I had it—breast cancer, Stage IIB—and all the barbaric treatments that go along with it. Surgery, chemo, radiation and hormone therapy saved my life. However, friends attributed my survival to determination, a positive outlook, and adoption of complementary treatments like juicing and acupuncture. After some doctors told me that chemo would leave me infertile, I even had a healthy baby without fertility assistance. I emerged from cancer triumphant. Friends and colleagues lauded me like a hero, and I let them. But, all of that was more than twice Stanley's lifetime ago, eight years in the distant past. And, indeed, Stanley wouldn't know what cancer is if it weren't for the lymphedema in my frighteningly-swollen left arm, perpetually wrapped in a giant compression cast.

Years after my cancer treatments were behind me and Stanley was toddling around, my forearm and hand unexpectedly swelled over a few days, to a 50% increase in size. My oncologist ordered a round of diagnostic scans. He framed it as, "looking for a resolution to the swelling." Not until he called me with the results did I realize that he was testing me for a cancer recurrence. He was audibly relieved when he shared that my scans were clear. We went on to discuss next steps, and my stomach sank as I realized that the doctor who saved my life had nothing in his medical toolbox to reverse the swelling. "Compression and physical therapy are the standard of care. There is no cure," he reported. As I discussed my scans and new treatments with family and close friends, we relived my entire cancer history within earshot of little Stanley. He asked to see where the doctors cut me open. I cannot feel where his little hand traced the scar: the nerves are gone there, leaving a numbness.

Every morning before work, my husband wrapped the compression cast around my arm while Stanley ate breakfast and watched this thirty-minute routine. First, a gauze stocking was carefully rolled over my lotioned skin. Then came layers of batting in a spiral, first one direction and then the other. My fingers received an intricate lacing of gauze that wove across the back of my hand, preventing the compression cast from driving fluid into my fingers. My husband, a former bicycle mechanic, joked that it was "just like wrapping handlebar tape." His tension and spacing was even and regular, as he wound the flesh colored short-stretch compression bandages in opposing upward spirals, creating a herringbone effect. The end-product of the wrapping job immobilized my elbow and was about the diameter of our breakfast plates. I was unable to wear shirts, jackets, or any clothing with sleeves. Sleeveless tops and ponchos became my new uniform.

At my physical therapist's urging, I tried wearing the compression cast round-the-clock. This caused my skin to develop sores, and the swelling to increase again. Each time I slept in the cast, I woke up, repeatedly, with my heart pumping in my ears. In my nightmares, I was being buried alive. I stopped sleeping in the cast, but then, my arm was more swollen each morning. Every evening at bedtime, we spent twenty minutes just rolling the bandages back into little tubes, tucking them away for the night. Stanley always helped by rolling one or two into a tangled ball. I re-rolled them after he was asleep. When our little family went out to eat Ethiopian, Stanley called the rolls of spongy injera bread "bandage bread."

Stanley also accompanied me to many of my twice-weekly physical therapy appointments. He was always quiet and polite while the therapist tried to break up the scar tissue and fibrosis that runs from my ribs, through my armpit, down to my wrist. She used her thumbs to push the fluids lodged in my arm back into my torso. When I dropped Stanley off at pre-school in my giant cast, he motioned in my direction and explained to his playmates "My mommy got a water arm!" He seemed at ease with my abnormality, and I marveled at the resilience of young children.

A few months into this routine, Stanley was alone with my husband when he broke down again. "Mommy not getting any better. We help and help, Daddy, and her water arm not better." They cried together.

At work, my colleagues assumed the cast was a result of a skiing or cycling accident. I tried to gloss over the cause of my cast and my frequent work absences for scans and physical therapy. My scientist and engineer coworkers were not satisfied with my vague explanation of a mysterious swelling. When I awkwardly explained that it is a latent side effect of cancer treatment, these smart folks, so used to solving problems, tried to solve my lymphedema. I had the same ridiculous conversations over and over again:

"How much longer?" "You mean in the cast? Or, until it's better? Oh. Well, it's considered chronic, incurable. A managed condition."

"It's called lymphedema. It's a swelling of the lymphatic system."

"No. It's not a new cancer. You might be thinking of lymphoma."

"Actually, it isn't that rare. About thirty percent of cancer patients get it. Usually it's happens to much older people. Lots of people here at work have moms who have it. Like Jon, and Barbara, and Lou."

"Yeah. Their moms are all in their seventies and eighties."

"Oh, well I wish it were my right arm instead, actually. See, I'm left handed."

"No, there's no medication for it. There are some experimental surgeries, but they aren't widely available."

"No. They can't just take out the fluid with a syringe. It's not localized fluid, plus the damage from the needle would only increase the swelling."

"No. My doctor hasn't asked me to keep it elevated. It just doesn't do much."

"Yes. It's painful. It throbs. Sometimes, it feels like the skin will split open. The pressure inside makes my fingers go numb."

"Well, actually, when the pain gets better, it means the tissue damage has become permanent."

"You are right. At least it isn't cancer."

After four months of bandaging, my lymphedema therapist announced that I could enter the maintenance phase. My left arm is still one-third larger than the right, and I cannot wear most long sleeve garments. I still need weekly physical therapy. The fabric on the over-the-counter compression sleeves buckled and chafed the skin, causing a rash that makes the swelling worse. I met with a medical device fitter. For $1200, I bought something called a "night garment." It is custom-made and looks like a shoulder-length oven mitt. I also got a made-to-measure sleeve and glove in nude, at $500 a set. They were made in Germany and came with my surname printed inside and a personal note from someone named Hulya, who inspected them. My Cadillac PPO health policy says that none of it is covered by insurance because "compression hosiery" are "personal items." I will need a new glove and sleeve every three months, for life. I tried to calculate the lifetime cost, and thought of college for Stanley. Even with daily hand-washing, the sleeve and glove quickly became grimy and stained from pencil, ink, riding the bus, cooking, and hanging out with a preschooler. Within a month, I also bought a black on black set. Stanley was delighted, "Mommy, now you Darth Mommy." I reached after him with my black hand, making breathing sounds, "Stanley....I am your mother. Join me and together we will rule the universe!"

Often, while I am doing my home exercises for lymphedema, my mind plays a running list: Things I Could Have Done Differently to Keep from Getting LYMPHEDEMA. I should not have worked such long hours. I should not have gotten so stressed out. I should have lost the baby weight after Stanley. I should have eaten better. I should have drank less beer. I should not have tried to be a weekend warrior when I was so out of shape, overwhelming my lymphatic system. I should have said "no" to that second lymph node surgery during treatment, when I thought a hardened little lump in my underarm was a new cancer. When my left implant failed after radiation, I should not have worked with that overly-aggressive surgeon who widened my reconstruction incision into my armpit. Now, when I lie down, the whole implant rolls into my underarm, leaving my breast a hollow cavity and blocking any circulation in my underarm.

So many things could have been the culprit that led to my lymph fluid pressure exceeding the threshold in my arm, causing damage to nodes and vessels and resulting in a backup of lymph fluid that further damaged nodes and vessels, causing more backup of lymph fluids and creating the chain reaction that is lymphedema. I try to quiet my mind from the running list by laying it quietly next to its companion, another list that lies mostly dormant nowadays: Things I Could Have Done Differently to Keep from Getting CANCER. Stanley wanders by while I am stretching and stroking my arm. Suddenly, he asks, "When can I have a baby sister?" It is my turn to burst into tears. The acute flare-up of lymphedema was, most likely, caused by the hormonal crash that followed the miscarriage of my second pregnancy. The dramatic and sudden swelling came only a few days after I lost the baby at eight weeks. Losing a baby and gaining a ruined arm sometimes feels like bad luck, and other times, like I was too greedy, wanting a second child after cancer.

Once, I tried going half a day without the compression sleeve. It took three weeks to calm the resulting flare-up. I love cooking elaborate dishes for friends and family, which requires going a couple of hours without the glove. Afterward, my hand looks like a baby's hand: dimples where the knuckles should be, puffy, no definition of veins or tendons. Even with my compression garments on, each day I feel the sensation of my arm growing tight and slowly filling with fluid. Not only is lymphedema incurable and requiring constant maintenance, but it is also progressive. Any minute damage to the skin—a slip of the knife, an oven burn, bug bite, sunburn, paper cut, or rough cuticle—can become the incident that triggers a new flare-up, another permanent enlargement, or the dreaded cystitis, an infection that can lead to amputation or death.

No longer the hero who triumphantly beat cancer, I am now visibly maimed by it. Just as I fear a cancer recurrence, I fear that, to have saved my life from cancer, I must live without the enjoyable use of my arm. By trying to give Stanley a sibling, have I made myself less of a mother? How will I teach him to camp and hike when a bout of poison oak for me could end in amputation? Will I ever be able to take him backpacking? He'll never remember me before lymphedema, when I was strong and unafraid to play in the wild. Now I wear my fears on my sleeve.

What My Eyes See at the Bookstore

Mary Ladd

Pre-cancer, I used to do energetic things like walk the San Francisco streets for miles, without a care. Now, after cancer, I find it completely acceptable to collapse from exhaustion on the floor of a bookstore with my family nearby. The kids' corner is cool and contained, and I can sit on the wooden floor and rest while my son, Cipriano, reads to himself and my husband, Oscar, putters in the fiction aisle.

Cipriano wants me to hear details of an adorable book called *If You Give a Pig a Pancake*. I try to muster interest, but I'm frustrated with myself for being blocks away from home, and not pre-empting this fatigue by being snuggled up in bed. I feel winded even though we have only been out and about for an hour, buying some fruit and hanging out at a sunny playground. There, I sat and watched Cipriano run around and heard the squeals and yells from children—he knows to ask Oscar to chase him, because I am no longer able to run around outside the way I used to. Back on the floor, I nod when Cipriano looks at me, since he is waiting for a response to his story. But, my brain is not wrapping around the story or him. I love pancakes and reading, but this neighborhood excursion is not working out so well.

I am beginning to realize that I get myself in physical trouble by pushing, pushing, pushing myself to do the same things I did before cancer. My energy is not back one hundred percent, and it may take another six months or longer to return. Whenever I try to assign a timeline to finishing chemo, surgeries and treatments, and fully recovering, it is just an illusion, since my body is taking longer to rest and heal after so much medical trauma and drama. Other sickies likely know that timelines that are firmly attached to strict dates are pretty much full of false hope, what with things like infections popping up and getting in the way.

Part of my frustration and sadness is seeing that I am weak and tired. Instead of feeling strong and capable of doing routine physical and mental tasks (I see you, Excel spreadsheets! And even responding to Cipriano's presentation of pig and pancakes at the book store!), I have to really talk myself into getting into the car to go on regular errands, or feign excitement at making eggs for breakfast.

On the floor of the bookshop, I perk up when I spot a *Vanity Fair* in the magazine aisle, straight across from where I'm sitting. I squint at the magazines because they are seven feet away and things are fuzzy without my glasses. I recently found out that I now need to wear glasses: my poor peepers were decimated by twenty-two rounds of chemo, and at one point during chemo, I was told I may have herpes in my eyes (not the sex-related kind of herpes). I cried when the eye doctor showed pictures of my eye glands, because even though I am just forty, my eyes could belong to someone who is seventy-five or older. Also, my lowered immunity from cancer means the severe red swollen eye bumps will continue to pop up when I am tired and stressed. Which is, you know, every few days. The broken down eye glands are another sign that life is just tougher after getting dealt the cancer and BRCA1 gene mutation cards.

Next to the *Vanity Fair* is a 'zine called *Wigs*. It looks colorful and fun, with ladies in costumes from different historical eras. I ask Oscar to add *Wigs* and *Vanity Fair* to our stash when he ambles over. When I am finally in bed a few hours later, I am warm with happiness and the prospect of reading a 'zine called *Wigs*. Gazing at wigs while I'm snuggled in bed solo reflects my new normal and gives me great ideas on ways to dress up my tired and ailing self.

Dark Night of the Soul

Naked Heart

Looking for the light

In the softness of the night

Turmoil churns my insides

While in silence it abides

Clawing out of the pit

Waiting for night to pass

In gentleness it flashes

Lighting up my past

Stories of old stir alive

People long dead now vying

For attention, I'd rather not give

In this moment I can't live

Distracting myself with distraction

Fatal is the TV's attraction

Losing myself in wine and cheese

Give me a break, please

The cover of night passes

Morning sun at last rescues

Another burning of my soul

I'm lighter and more whole

In a Hurry

Janet S.

I want to see, touch, do, taste, smell, feel everything. I want to go everywhere, walk the earth, climb the mountains and snowboard down. Try everything at least once.

Lots to do, I'm in a hurry. Not much time left. How long do I have before the cancer makes it impossible? Narrows the world to just my room, my doctor's office, the hospital? I don't know, I can't know.

Time wasted planning for a future I don't have. Working to save for a family I will never have. No more, I'm here now to experience everything. To dance and sing and laugh around the world and at home.

But, I can't do it all. No lifetime is enough to experience everything. To watch the sunrise from space.

I will see, touch, do, taste, smell, feel everything I can. In my lifetime, however long or short it may be. And it will be enough.

Longing to Leave

Merijane Block

I long to leave. Easily, quickly, with little to no preparation. To go from pajamas into jeans and an old friendly sweatshirt, my feet slipped into clogs or flip-flops, a quick brush through my hair—or not—a swoosh of clear gloss on my lips.

A satchel over one shoulder, with room to spare for what I may pick up or simply find along the way. My keys in my pocket, a basket in one hand, in case a farmers market floats by in my line of vision.

I long to leave with only ten minutes' notice. Because I have decided I want an afternoon movie and one near my house starts in twenty-five minutes. Because a friend across town wants to have dinner together, or needs me to take *her* to the doctor or even, heaven help us, to the nearest emergency room. Because I can.

I long to leave. My bed, immediately upon waking, to *jump*—as they say, as I *used* to say—or to *hop* into the shower. Leave my bed, to turn on the kettle and brew a whole pot of tea, because I will drink it all while I do what many do in the morning, what I once could do—race around and get things done, a satisfying end in itself, all that doing.

I long to leave and travel light. No cane, for starters. No extra sweater or scarf for the inevitable fog coming over later in the day. So what if I'm cold? I'll just move faster. Because I can. Or I'll dash home—*dash*—and up the three flights and pick up what I need later. Quickly, happily, gratefully, maybe, but more than likely, not so mindfully. Simply because I can. Because I am able.

I long to leave it until later, because I know I'll have the energy to do it—all the its. Not because I'm waiting for the possible arrival of an extra burst.

I long to leave behind the necessary premeditation. To lay aside the near-constant anxiety that precedes the beginning of almost anything. The exhaustion of all that preparation, physical and mental.

I long to leave this body the way a snake leaves its skin, to shed the constraints of my restrictions, real and learned, and tread lightly across the landscapes, as it was once so effortless to do.

"Longing to Leave" previously appeared online at *Birdland Journal, Work by Laguna Writers,* December 15, 2015.

V. ABSURDITIES

"Under certain circumstances, urgent circumstances, desperate circumstances, profanity provides a relief denied even to prayer."

— Mark Twain, in *Mark Twain: A Biography*,
by Albert Bigelow Paine

"Reality was one step out of line,
a cardigan with the buttons done up wrong."

— Haruki Murakami, *Sputnik Sweetheart*

Side Eye

Cat Huegler

No one knows how to deal with cancer. No one! It makes us all say really crazy things, even with the best intentions in mind. Looking back, we can see the humor.

Here are eight of the most misguided things people said to me. While I gave all of them the side eye, I did not slap a single one. It's a small miracle.

1. "Oh, no, I'm so sorry! Our neighbor just died of breast cancer."

   A co-worker, upon finding out I was just diagnosed with breast cancer.

2. "Where does it hurt?"

   The nurse, when I complained about pain after my double mastectomy surgery. You should have seen my husband's frustrated and stunned reaction.

3. "No shit!?! You used to be hot."

   A co-worker who saw a picture of me with long hair, taken before chemo.

4. "I am so sick of going to doctor's appointments! Go here, go there. When will I feel better!?!"

    A clueless friend with the flu.

5. "Aim for a handful."

    My plastic surgeon, to my husband (who, by the way, is 6'6" with extra huge hands), when discussing reconstruction size.

6. "You have to have chemo? Good, maybe you'll lose weight and get super skinny! Yay!"

    A friend?

7. "Oh my god, I am so, so, so, soooo tired. I had to work two days this week. I'm so tired that I'm nauseous. I'm so tired I could sleep for a week!"

    A co-worker, said with a straight face, as I sat there bald and bloated, between rounds three and four of chemo, after working a full work week.

8. "So, you are ok now, right?"

    Everyone, ever.

…Side Eye

Transcendence

Erika Gee

When the radiologist left me a message on Monday afternoon and asked me to call her to find out my biopsy results, I procrastinated. I was confident the findings were going to be nothing, so I just went on with my life, ate pizza with co-workers, and watched *12 Years a Slave*. Confronting the terrible treatment of multi-generations of enslaved peoples and its lasting legacy for the country, while it left me deeply depressed, somehow seemed a better use of time than learning my biopsy results.

The next day, I called the radiologist back. The news: breast cancer. It was too much to watch that movie about slavery *and* be told I had cancer within the same twenty-four hours. I was already reeling from the stark brutality, injustice, and continued effects of slavery. I was at work and needed some place private to let this all wash over me, so I went into a closet to cry. A lot. I felt powerless from the weight of institutional trauma. I felt helpless to take care of myself. The movie showed me about how life can get taken away— was my life going to get taken away, in a different way, too? In some ways, procrastination saved me a day of terrible news, but what I chose to do with that borrowed time set me up in an emotional mayhem.

But, I had to pick myself up and figure out next steps. I was only three months into a new job. Should I tell people I had cancer? What happens if I do? Or I don't? I was going to need time off from work even though I did not want to be known as a "bad worker." Yet, since I had just started the job, I hadn't accrued sick or vacation time. I thought that I could take time off on short-term disability and so went ahead and scheduled my lumpectomy. But, while I was recovering from my surgery, I learned that my claim was denied. I hadn't worked in California for the prior six months, so I didn't qualify for state disability. And, my workplace didn't have an extended leave policy for employees who had been there less than a year. With further treatment looming, there would be more, necessary, time-off. But, could I take that time off for the seemingly-unending treatments *and* have no income? It seemed like my choices went from bad to worse and I was becoming a slave to some ill-conceived "policies" that clearly lacked humanity too!

With limited options, I returned to work. In the midst of trying to perform my duties, juggling doctors' appointments, and crying a lot, I tried to hold it together, with a sense of agency being my only salve. I researched pooled sick-leave policies. I called other HR managers. I visited so many other nonprofit and for-profit websites. Armed with some examples, I proposed solutions to my managers.

When that fell on deaf ears, my co-workers came to my rescue, starting a campaign and advocating on my behalf. Besides just helping me, I hoped that this would set a precedent for more employee-friendly and humane policies, especially for those with catastrophic diagnoses like cancer, and especially given the sad irony that the mission of my employer is to promote equity and social justice in the world, yet it was failing to put these values into practice with their own employees.

While my managers decided not to institute a pooled sick leave policy, a few senior managers donated their sick leave to me. Because of this, after my second surgery, a mastectomy because my margins weren't clear from the lumpectomy, I was able to get three weeks of paid sick leave—three whole, stress-free weeks to rest and recover with a completely new body. And, during my many months of chemotherapy, my supervisor got approval to hire additional help, so that if I had to take time off, I didn't have to worry that my work wouldn't be completed. These accommodations would not have happened without my co-workers and their championing my circumstances.

From the very beginning of this experience, remembering those raw emotions both after watching *Twelve Years a Slave* and learning about my breast cancer diagnosis, I know that there is a lot of hurt in the world and terrible history that we can't change.

But, my co-workers, now friends, were willing to put themselves out there, to bolster me. They are a continued reminder that whatever hardships I face, that the world faces, that we are not alone in our struggles.

And, while my life with cancer has, at times, been hard to watch, just like *Twelve Years a Slave*, my eyes are opened to the grace and transcendence that is possible.

Lost in the Fog

Jill Sakol Snow

I was sitting in the tranquil lobby at SenSpa in the San Francisco Presidio when my cell phone buzzed. It was a text message from my dog walker letting me know that my gentle, spry Dalmatian mutt, Pepper, was acting strangely. The dog was disoriented and having difficulty walking. She was an older dog who had been part of our family for eleven years, so this change in behavior was very concerning. I asked the dog walker to take Pepper to the vet immediately.

I, too, had been feeling disoriented. A week ago, I received the phone call from my oncologist that altered my state of mind. After over four years with no evidence of disease, my breast cancer had likely returned. The radiologist who read my last PET scan wasn't even sure what kind of cancer I had, as it was showing up in my bones and lymph nodes and not again in my breast. A chest lymph node biopsy was planned for the next day. My mom had brought me to the spa for some relaxation to be followed by a leisurely lunch at a nearby café.

At the restaurant, we chatted casually to keep me distracted from my bigger worries, when the vet called with news of Pepper's condition, which he described as most likely marijuana intoxication. They could send her blood to a lab for an expensive test to confirm, but the vet didn't think this was needed, as they see this condition often in San Francisco, and can easily identify the symptoms. His recommendation was to keep the dog overnight for treatment and observation.

Our poor Pepper was stoned out of her mind.

How did that happen? I knew she didn't get it from me, but what about that nanny I just hired? Would the vet be required to file a police report? Would I arrive home from my relaxing day to face questions from the authorities about how my dog was poisoned? Would she make a complete recovery?

That evening, I gathered my two boys, ages seven and four years, together for a talk in their cozy shared bedroom. I had not yet told them that my cancer had recurred as there were still so many unanswerable questions. I wanted to protect them from the fear and uncertainty that was hanging over me, but I needed to share some information about tomorrow's procedure. "Mommy is sick," I said. "It is a sickness that is inside my body. I need to have a test that will help the doctors to figure out what kind of medicine will help to make me better, and this test will be done in a hospital tomorrow morning. I will come home after the test is all finished."

The cloud of silence that hung over the room for several moments was quickly interrupted by my older son who demanded, "WHERE IS PEPPER?" I was flabbergasted. This was their first and most pressing question?

I explained that Pepper was very sick and needed to spend the night at the veterinarian's office. Immediately, they both burst into tears. "We can't go to sleep without the dog here," they cried. "When will she get better?" "What is the vet doing to her?" So many questions about THE DOG! I thought that maybe their concern about Pepper's health kept them from worrying about me, so I accepted their questions with patience. I held them in my arms, and, eventually, they calmed down and were able to go to sleep.

I went to the hospital the next morning, as planned, but right away, things did not go as expected. My oncologist had pulled some strings to get me scheduled for this biopsy as soon as possible, and he confirmed that the senior doctor in the department would perform my procedure. My parents, my husband Scott, and I met with a hospital intern who explained the procedure to us, including the risks. We were horrified to learn that because the incision would be made through my back and into the middle of my chest, there was a risk of lung puncture. Not to worry, the intern said, as a few days in the hospital would heal up the lung.

What? Was he joking? Was it really possible to have so many bad things happen to one person in one week? Cancer, a critically-ill dog, a painful procedure, and now, possibly, a deflated lung— wouldn't that be the icing on the cake?!

My family tried to cheer me up in the waiting room. My husband even pulled up a YouTube video of a *Simpsons* episode about Homer Simpson experiencing the five stages of grief in rapid succession when he thinks he is dying from eating poisonous sushi. Their attempts worked, somewhat, with a few minutes of comic relief, especially in comparison to poor Pepper and her pot consumption.

Finally, the nurse called me in to the treatment room where I met the attending physician. "Wait", I asked, "where is the senior doctor who would be doing my procedure?" The attending replied, "He is not available. The intern will be doing your procedure under my supervision." I was petrified and wanted to leave. However, this test was too important to reschedule, so I dug deeply with the hope that these doctors-in-training knew what they were doing.

For this procedure, the doctors use a CT scanner to guide where they put the long, thin needle into my back to take the tissue sample. The process is very slow as doctors need to keep checking their positioning. They even push the lungs out of the target range using injections of saline solution, which explains why I felt like I had swallowed a swimming pool. I had to be awake to follow special breathing instructions, so they applied only a local anesthetic, and did so slowly, too slowly, as they had to briefly stop in the middle of the procedure when I nearly passed out from the pain. I laid there with what was essentially a giant knitting needle sticking out of my back, feeling like I was drowning and struggling to stay conscious, fog creeping in and around my line of vision. Finally, they got their sample and the ordeal was over.

I fully came to in the recovery room with Scott by my side. He had been in contact with the vet's office to get updates on Pepper. Thankfully, she made a complete recovery out of her fog and was ready to come home. We never discovered how she ingested the marijuana, but she was known to smell and taste some pretty stinky waste that is found on the city streets.

Safely and comfortably recovering together at home, Pepper and I laid near each other in my bedroom. My boys rejoiced to have our dog safely home again, while my parents kept them occupied so I could have time to rest. I began to heal from from the painful effects of the biopsy, and my initial fog began to recede, fog that surrounded me, which, I believe, served to protect my mind and soul from the painful shock of learning about my breast cancer recurrence. During this time, I learned that a complete recovery from metastatic breast cancer is not assured or likely possible.

Over a few weeks spent reviewing treatment options, I grappled with my fear. I finally realized late one night, after studying certain research articles about Western and Eastern medicine, that we all live with fear. When fear can be recognized for what it is in its most simple form (i.e., "It is fear"), it shrinks and becomes less frightening, more transparent. I realized that it didn't matter if the first treatment I tried didn't work, or made me feel awful, that I had options and could try something else.

For the first time in weeks, I felt clear-minded and ready to face whatever was coming next. Most importantly, I still had my family and Pepper with me for support.

Now, more than three years later, we all are still together, sometimes in the fog of cancer, but more often outside and enjoying the light of day, even in foggy San Francisco.

Parking for Chemo

Emily Kaplan

Samara gave me her fairy dust necklace as a good luck charm for all my chemo days. My spirits are high, Stephany and I are laughing, making jokes about rashes in interesting places on our bodies, and rocking out to songs on the radio.

Because I have a handicap placard, we search for a metered space so we don't have to pay the $12 for valet parking. We turn on to Post Street and don't see any spaces, but I see someone get into his car. I motion to him to ask if he's leaving; he is. I hop out of the car to stand in the empty space while Stephany makes a U-turn, but there's road construction, so she needs to circle the block. I start to cross the street, and a speeding taxi cab honks his horn and wildly hand motions to me while muttering to himself.

The man in the car behind the taxi yells out the open window, "You stupid fucking bitch!" as I jog to stand in the empty metered space. I turn, slack-jawed, and try to give him an evil stare as he's driving away.

While I am standing in the space, a woman pulls up and asks what I'm doing. I say that I'm saving the space. She says, "You're not allowed to save spaces." I say, "Well, I'm doing it."

A second woman pulls up in a black Suburban. She looks at me and said, "Are you taking that space?" I say "Yes." She rolls her eyes and pulls away.

Then, a small man in a small VW convertible pulls up and asks me if I'm saving this space. I say, "Yes." He says, "You're not allowed to. I don't know any place that allows you to hold a space." I say, "Well, I'm doing it anyway." He says, "Well, people need these spaces." I say, "I do too. I have a chemo appointment." He says, "I have a doctor's appointment." I say, "Which one wins: chemo or doctor's appointment?" He is fuming; he turns on his hazard lights, deciding how far to take the argument.

Luckily, I see Stephany coming up the street in my Prius. The small VW man puts his car in reverse and begins backing up while I'm standing in the empty space. I motion to Stephany to pull in the space nose first as he's also trying to back in.

We win.

He makes a U-turn and finds a space across the street. We go into the Cancer Center. We get in the elevator going to the fifth floor when I notice the sign on the elevator numbers, that the fourth floor is for Anal Dysplasia. "Could be worse," I say.

When I Was Tina Turner

Sia Sellu

When I was first diagnosed with breast cancer, everyone was talking about my hair. I am a black woman in America, so a lot of talk is about hair—too short, too nappy, too unnatural, too natural, to weave or not to weave. After learning that I needed chemo, I figured that I would be fine as a bald woman. I mean, I had spent the last few years wearing wigs and headwraps, after securing proper stylists and braiders proved elusive in my Pacific Northwest town.

As I started chemo, I thought I would have some time to get used to my hair G-R-A-D-U-A-L-L-Y falling out. So, a few days after my first chemo, as I was sitting at the bar, taking a small meal and sipping a Manhattan—just doing what I could to get through!—I ran my hand through my hair, and that hand held a huge, dusty bunny of my kinky, curly hair. What the fuck?

Resolved to take control and with an image of a strong, bald woman in my mind, I went home and shaved my head. There weren't many tears involved. I was way more disturbed by the ugly port that delivered my chemo, protruding from my chest, and I could only focus on one thing at a time.

I wrapped my newly-bald head in the same beautiful head wraps I always had, and on my way I went.

Silly me, though, I should have known that much as it had been my entire life, my hair or lack thereof was everybody else's concern. It started young, when my mother used to twist the small piece of my hair and bobby pin a little ribbon to it, so that people would know I was a girl. And here I was, a grown woman, now without hair, and everybody's focus on my hair aesthetics continued.

The chemo nurse at the fancy breast care center recommended that I see a volunteer about a wig. As it often took hours to get my chemo cocktail ready, I submitted to her suggestion, if only to kill time. I went into the donated wig room, which was staffed by what appeared to be nineteen-year-old, straight-identified male. My initial thought, "Um, Sia, don't judge, hair is *his* gift."

I was quick to learn: it wasn't his gift.

He had an assortment of wigs, which could all be summed up like this: little old white lady pixie cuts. Coupled with my rather large melon of a head, the wigs were not the desired, pretty result. I was annoyed, the kid was anxious, and we ended it right there.

The next day, I came back to the chemo room for my post-chemo Neupogen shot to boost my immune system. The medical assistant was beside himself, "Oh, we have a surprise for you!" He could barely control his giddy self. I was not giddy, though, as I waited to receive the shot I hate. But, I decided to oblige him.

I followed him back to the wig room, among the other staff who were asking, excitedly, "Has she seen it, yet?" I'll admit that my hopes were slightly raised.

The nurse said, "No, they haven't found a cure for cancer. But, they have found a wig that is perfect for you! And, a retired hairstylist is there to help you try it on! OH MY GAWD, can you believe it?" Um, no. I didn't really care either. But, they were all so happy about this damn wig, that I was like, "Ok, I'll try the thing on."

The retired hairstylist greeted me, "I have something for you. It is very Tina Turner, "Proud Mary" era." Really, people? Well, at least Tina *is* black.

Everyone gathered around the door, as the hairstylist put this dark auburn wig on my head and proceeded to take her time brushing, styling and spraying the wig. My audience of medical professionals was so happy, like they were witnessing a real live makeover show.

I spun around and eyeballed the mirror. The wig was pretty, sort of, but it was NOT me. Nevertheless, I wore it home because I didn't want to hurt anyone's feelings.

That night, a friend was having his birthday at a local bar (another Manhattan, please, after this day!). I wore my wig.

It was HOT AS HELL. I kept trying to channel Ms. Tina, but instead, I felt like I had a hot-ass hat on my head.

Finally, a friend said, "Please take that off...You are so uncomfortable that, you're making us uncomfortable." I took it off, ran outside and threw it in my car trunk.

From then on, I rocked the bald head. Uncomfortable for them, comfortable for me.

Look Good, Feel Shitty

Laurie Hessen Pomeranz

When I was diagnosed with Stage IIB breast cancer in 2010, I was forty-one-years old. Whenever asked what my stage was cancer was when I found my lump and was diagnosed, I say "Two B." My reflective thought after that is, "Two B or not to be." Because, that is the question. That is what we all ask ourselves when we are diagnosed with cancer. Am I going to FUCKING DIE?

My son was just seven. We have no family history of breast cancer, and the diagnosis came as a massive shock. I proceeded to undergo a mastectomy, chemotherapy, radiation, reconstruction, multiple hospitalizations for infections and failed reconstruction, daily hormone therapy of Tamoxifen, and then the aromatase inhibitor Letrazole. Now, I get infusions for the osteoporosis caused by all of this hormone deprivation.

One day, early on in the process, I was at my oncologist's office and read about an event for cancer patients. It was being held at The Ritz, so seemed like a good excuse to get out of my sweats and go have some cancer-related fun (what an oxymoron). I grabbed a couple of my new breast cancer sisters, and we went together. We looked forward to some yummy snacks and pampering from the "Look Good, Feel Better" team, who were going to offer us makeovers and products to hopefully help us look a little less pallid and devoid of eyebrows.

Circled up around large tables in a Ritzy conference room, my girlfriends and I were surrounded by other women with breast cancer and a large crew of volunteer make-up artists who were there to take care of us. The room was abuzz in friendly banter and enthusiastic anticipation. Then, the bags of cosmetics were handed out, and my mood turned from upbeat to astonished. What the hell was this shit they were handing me?

The American Cancer Society was about to "pamper us" with donated products from a major cosmetics company, that contained synthetic fragrance, parabens and god-knows what else. Why were they giving cancer patients known endocrine-disruptors, which mimic estrogen and can be carcinogenic? I was in active treatment for highly estrogen-sensitive breast cancer. I was cutting out estrogen-mimicking compounds everywhere I could, in what I put in and on my body. I was on medication to block my breast cells from binding to estrogen. Then, I go to a cancer-related event, intended to support me, and was given this chemical crap? It made absolutely zero sense to me, and I got pissed.

I called over one of the cosmetologists and said, "There is fragrance in these products!" She responded, "Oh, we only use the highest quality ingredients." I replied, "All of these products have fragrance and parabens, which we all try to avoid," (At that time, I was on Tamoxifen and didn't even realize the additional issue: these toxic chemicals are thought to interfere with Tamoxifen's effectiveness.).

The irony and hypocrisy of the situation got me into a minor fury. I decided that I needed to just leave. My friends walked out with me. We went out for a lovely dinner instead. Much safer and less enraging. The happiness that comes with quality girl-time makes me "look better" than any penciled-on eyebrows do, anyway.

The next day, I called the organizer of the event and shared my concern about the dangerous products they were handing-out to cancer patients. The organizer was courteous (though clueless), and said she would "pass along my feedback."

Two years later, I was hospitalized, twice, for a total of eighteen days, to cope with infections in my breast reconstruction. Eventually, I lost the implant, when the infection could not be managed. On the seventh day in the hospital, when all my IV tubing was removed and changed out, they let me have my first real shower. This was not the kind of shower that involved the tenderness of my husband washing my hair in the hospital bathroom sink, but the kind where I actually got to stand, naked and free, no IV pole, no tubing, no needles, and luxuriate in a hot shower.

I was given a towel and a little bag of products, and directed to the private stall at the end of the hospital corridor. When I opened that bag of bath products—there they were again! Pink, green, highly-fragranced, crap products. Stuff I won't let my child use, stuff I won't use on myself, stuff that is full of all the ingredients that I try to avoid, because they aren't good for any of us. There I was, in the hospital, dealing with complications from highly-estrogenic breast cancer, and the hospital was handing this stuff out? Really?

That was six years ago. I just heard from another BAYS sister who attended the "Look Good, Feel Better" event this year that the same cosmetics company is still providing the makeovers and products. The same toxic personal care products and cosmetics are still being doled out to cancer patients, in the name of looking good and feeling better.

I would expect the American Cancer Society and the hospital system to be part of the solution, not another one of the chemical shitstorm perfume-peddlers. Come on, people. You can do better than that. And, I won't stop flapping my jaw about it until you do.

The Vacation

Kara Carter

It's 7pm, and I am staring at the blank, grey wall of a hospital room, trying to work out how I got here. Not so much in an existential way (although that would actually be valid—this is not the life I imagined for myself at 'just-turned-thirty-nine'), but in a literal way. How did I end up in a hospital bed tonight? And, more importantly, can I leave in the morning?

I look around. There isn't much to see. The bed, the slightly grimy looking walls, an ancient cathode ray TV perched so high I couldn't watch it even if it did work. The bulletin board next to the computer holds a reminder to WASH YOUR HANDS, together with a couple of other notes for nurses and family members (or "caregivers"). Something about its overprotective authority reminds me of primary school. It's almost cozy, in a way. A sharp contrast to the clinical beeping, flashing IV machine that tethers me to the bed.

I try to fight off a pang of depression with pragmatism. I'm good at pragmatism, and even I know that a temperature of 101° is not ok, especially not two weeks after my first chemo. After a weekend of failed attempts to address the fever on my own, I gave in two hours ago, and phoned the doctor. Now, I'm in a hospital bed, tubes of antibiotics running into the crook of my arm.

The source of infection is obvious; my left breast, halfway through reconstruction, is an ugly deep purple, a size bigger than it should be, and hot to the touch. I had expected the phone call and subsequent clinic appointment to result in a simple prescription for antibiotics. Not this.

I realize I am in trouble when a look I don't recognize crosses the nurse's face, as she examines the eggplant that was once a boob. Less "Let's get you patched up and on your way," and more "Houston, we have a problem."

"Umm...I think we'd better get *him*," she says, her special emphasis on "him" letting me know she meant the surgeon. I am already reaching for my clothes and am mentally on my way home as this slowly sinks in. Fuck.

The next four hours brings multiple x-rays, probing examinations, a small procedure and, oh yeah, another post-surgical JP drain.

The fifth hour. Here I am, wondering how I got here.

My partner D arrives, with sushi, and I thank whatever fates remain loyal to my cause. By the time I was finally booked into my room, I had missed dinner. D also comes bearing other gifts: my iPad, a toothbrush, hairbrush and a hoodie. This grey room is oddly cold, and hospital-issued pajamas are somewhat drafty. I drape the hoodie over my shoulders, as the IV won't allow me to pull it on properly. Despite the additional warmth, I'm miserable.

I look at D mournfully, "Will you stay? Please?" He looks over his shoulder at the blue plastic chair, which allegedly unfolds to some kind of sleeping contraption, akin to an airplane in 1982. "Sure," he says with a smile which looks suspiciously like a grimace. "Of course I will." We eat sushi and watch Netflix while we wait for a nurse to change the drip bags dribbling a constant flow of antibiotics into my arm.

It's morning now. My plastic surgeon arrives. It seems I can expect to be here for five to seven days. Given everything the last three months has brought—diagnosis, surgery, chemo, biopsies, scans and what seems like a constant rotation of blood draws—this should seem like a minor setback. But, it doesn't feel that way. In my whole life to this point, I'd spent exactly one night in a hospital bed after the double mastectomy. I find myself feeling like I've somehow failed, and I'm frustrated. And then I find myself frustrated with my frustration, as if the emotion is a further failure. I can see nothing but disappointment, boredom, and enslavement to an IV pole stretching in front of me...for day upon day upon...

"Think of it like going on vacation," says D. I stare at him.

"Umm..."

"Really," he goes on, "it's not so bad. Someone will cook for you. You don't have to worry about work. You can read books, and we can watch movies."

"Seriously?"

"Sure," he says with an alarming degree of sincerity.

"Worst vacation ever!"

It's an in-joke, born of a nineties sitcom. "Worst birthday ever!" is our code for "hilariously bad, but could be worse." It's not my birthday though.

At 10am, a nutritionist turns up. I assume she's been told that (a) I will be here for a bit, and (b) I am a vegan. She stays for around half an hour, and in that time we engage in that half chat-half lecture, which was foreshadowed by the strident signage around the room. Apparently, as a vegan, I need to keep my protein levels up and should choose higher calorie options. I do wonder what all those calories will be used for since I can only shuffle in a three-foot circle around my IV pole. She leaves with the warning that supplemental shakes will need to be arranged if I can't get enough nutrition. A sense of threat in the statement suggests that the shakes will taste of sock-water.

While I am imagining this taste sensation, someone arrives with a weird tube to blow into, and a set of what can only be described as electronic leg warmers. I am told the former is to measure lung capacity since I am effectively bed bound. The latter is to prevent clotting. It's yet another mechanism tethering me to one place, and I'm not sure I can take this additional indignity, however small. I look beseechingly at the nurse:

"Do you really think I need these?"

"Well, it's standard for a stay this long."

"Why? I'm thirty-nine, not ninety. My blood still works. See?" I waggle my leg.

"Well...." her voice trails off.

I think she is still talking, but I can only focus on how miserable I am.

The rest of the afternoon passes in a kind of fugue state. I read, flip through magazines, have my vitals checked, and D and I try to squish awkwardly into the hospital bed to watch more Netflix. At one point, D pops out to the gift shop and comes back with teas and juices. This is basically the high point of my day. I used to do other things—work, travel, the hum of every day life, which seems somehow exotic and exciting to me as I stare out the gray window at the gray parking lot.

Three hours of Facebook later, a catering assistant arrives with dinner. It comes on a tray, the dishes complete with metal covers to keep the heat in. I imagine a fine dining establishment, where the waiter whips these off with a triumphant "Voilà!" I attempt to replicate this with the same degree of gusto, while simultaneously negotiating the spaghetti-trap of IV tubing.

My "Voilà" catches in my throat. It comes out as "Vvvvvvv." Under the cover, I see four spindly, boiled carrots. And…well, there is no "and." Four carrots. Four very small carrots, boiled to within an inch of their life. With a side of saltines.

D looks at me. He looks at the tray.

"Are those...carrots?"

"Ummmm. Yeah. I think so. And, um, tea. And saltines, I guess?"

"Wow."

"Room service sucks at this hotel, huh?"

"Yeah, I guess so. And now that I think about it, the view is kind of shitty too."

"And there is so much noise at night!"

"And all these people come in and keep interrupting. Terrible service."

"Like I said: Worst. Vacation. Ever."

Softly Floating

Robin Bruns Worona

Before cancer, when I did "normal" San Francisco-parent things, I took my twin toddlers to music class. The kids were basically still babies, so it was really the parents who did all the work, singing and dancing like idiots. There was this one song:

Leaves are falling, softly floating

Tumbling to the ground

If this were the movie about my breast cancer experience (hey, stranger things have happened!), it opens with that song and this scene:

Slow-mo, soft focus, close-up of bright, primary-colored balloons softly floating down, then gently popping back up and lightly bouncing off each other as the camera slowly pans out. Think the opening shower scene of Stephen King's Carrie, but with balloons.

As we pan out further, we see a circle of women, aged sixty to ninety, wearing ill-fitting wigs and jaunty "chemo caps." Laughing rather maniacally, they tap at the balloons. They are dressed in soft clothes, in even softer colors. Lilac sweatpants. Pale, chenille-ruffled cardigans. Entire Pepto Bismol-pink ensembles. One or two—the radicals—wear "Fuck Cancer" T-shirts.

In my movie, the internal monologue kicks in, something like this:

What. The. Fuck. Did these grannies all hit the medical Mary Jane right before class? Is this that "chemo brain" I've been hearing so much about? It's not bad enough that I puked this morning, can't stand up without feeling dizzy, my right arm is totally numb, my shin bones ache, my hips are screaming, and oh yeah, I have CANCER. Now I have to play with balloons? Wasn't this class called CORE workout or something?

I have not yet learned one of the most important lessons of cancer: it's ok, totally ok, to walk out.

I do not yet understand how exhaustingly busy the life of a cancer patient is. Doctor visits, blood work, heart scans, CT scans, PET scans, support groups, acupuncture, therapy, blog updates, phone calls with concerned friends and family, disability paperwork, and free CLASSES. Meditation classes, tai chi classes, nutrition classes, yoga classes, makeup (yes, I mean how to draw on *Mommy Dearest* eyebrows) classes! I have not yet realized that sometimes, often, actually, it's best to just skip it and take a nap.

My cancer diagnosis has sparked an internal struggle of epic proportions for me. I've never been a joiner. In fact, I've always had an aversion to joining groups. But, I am unable to resist free shit. So here I am, balloons and all.

Back to my movie, er, life.

The teacher gleefully chirps at us to form two lines. I realize, in horror, that we are about to play a series of line games with the balloons. A painful memory from elementary school surfaces—the yearly birthday party of a family friend who went to a different school. The rich kid school, to be exact. The parties were huge, raucous affairs, and always involved some sort of ACTIVITY. The worst being the "Year of the Neighborhood Scavenger Hunt." How was an eight-year-old supposed to know that a clover and a clove were not the same thing? The second worse, the "Year of the Line Games." Passing balloons between our legs and over our heads. Then, oranges held under our chins, with perky, petite girls—my diametrical opposites—who I didn't know at all, giggling while "necking" with each other to pass the oranges. Traumatizing.

Best yet for me, today's class is "extra full!" So, we are all wedged in together, like bald, pastel sardines. I notice the woman in front of me has on a sweater dress. A sweater dress! It looks damn comfortable. But, is it appropriate exercise attire? I have not yet learned one of the other most important lessons of cancer—fuck it.

When she bends over to pass the balloon between her legs, I have to squat awkwardly to retrieve it, so that my ass doesn't hit the woman's face behind me.

What the fuck am I doing here?

After class the ladies are flushed and chatty. The teacher introduces me—the highlights being that I have two-and-a-half-year-old twins and am having a really hard time with nausea. She asks them each to share a piece of advice with me. They smile and tell me how lucky I am that my kids are so young that they won't even remember this. They tell me to drink ginger tea. "Try those motion sickness wrist bands," one lady offers. They reach out and pat me. Hug me. I want to confess my mean thoughts, run away. I am SUCH a bitch.

But really, a sweater dress?

Flash forward a year. I have gotten through chemo, mastectomy, radiation. Months of shortness of breath and coughing from said radiation. Debilitating fatigue, endless alternating bouts of diarrhea and constipation. Hot flashes, blah blah blah, I could go on for hours. Let's just leave it at: lots of not-fun shit. Finally, I've had my reconstruction surgery, hopefully my final, in an arduous series of surgeries.

I am TIRED.

On a sunny Saturday afternoon, I find myself resting on the couch. The kids want to play. Exhausted, I look around the room and spot a couple of balloons leftover from a friend's birthday party. "Bring those over here," I say.

And so, I lie on the couch, tapping balloons back and forth with my kids, watching them floating softly to the ground. "Hey kids, you know what would be really great right now? Go get Mom her sweater dress."

End scene.

Cancer: A Haiku

Kara Carter

Facebook ads, last year:
Clothes, credit cards, cosmetics
This year: Medicare

Boob in an Envelope

Laurie Hessen Pomeranz

I am not the kind of person who reliably unpacks her suitcase on vacation. Sometimes, it's easier for me to just grab and go. When I go to Nantucket, however, I always unpack. It signifies that I get to stay awhile, slow down, take my time.

On last summer's trip to Nantucket to see my husband's family, Jeff and I got the big upstairs bedroom in the rental home. It had a lovely cottage-chic hutch for a dresser, with a tiny drawer at the top. It was the kind of drawer that may once have held doilies or cigars. Slim, secret, a little rickety. This narrow drawer seemed like the perfect home for Water Boob. Water Boob is the silicone breast prosthesis that fits into the pouch of my bathing suit when I go swimming. Every day upon returning home from the beach, I'd grab a nice hot shower, rinse my body and remaining breast, then wash and towel-off Water Boob and store her in the doily drawer.

When we left Nantucket at the end of that beautiful, festive family vacation, my husband, son and I headed back to San Francisco. Within a couple of days of being back home, we were heading to the beach with friends. I grabbed my bathing suit and went to grab Water Boob. But, she was nowhere to be found.

And then it hit me...she was seaside in Nantucket, in that toasty little drawer.

My friend from college writes songs for kids. One of them is called, "I Lost the Tooth I Lost." It tells the story of a kid who loses his tooth, and it goes flying across the floor, out the kitchen door. In the chorus, he laments, "I lost the tooth. I lost the tooth I lost." I found myself singing, "I lost the boob. I lost the boob I lost." I scrambled for any record of the name of the guy who rented us the house. I called my father-in-law. He told me to call our agent, Chip, at the rental firm in Nantucket.

I called and got Chip's voicemail. His outgoing message was sun-soaked, and, well, downright chipper. It was 6pm in Nantucket, and I imagined Chip was out of the office for the day. He was probably already sipping gin and tonics somewhere, in his flip flops and madras pants.

"Hi, Chip. It's Laurie Pomeranz. My father-in-law rented the house on Pochik this past week. I left something behind, and wonder if you can please give me a call? Thanks."

A day went by.

I left another message.

Another day went by. I was getting irritated. Did he think I was just another former renter calling about a forgotten pair of sunglasses? Was this dude blowing me off?

I called again. I decided to dial-up the seriousness.

"Hi, Chip. It's Laurie Pomeranz here, John Pomeranz's daughter-in-law. Sorry to bug you. I left something important and personal at the rental house last week. Can you please give me a call? Thank you."

I was getting myself into a lather at the lack of response, and at the thought of having to shell out another $300 if I couldn't get Water Boob back soon. It was summer time. I work in a school and was off for the summer. My child was off for the summer. We had plans! Insurance only pays for a new Water Boob every two years. Mine was new. She does wither over that two-year period. When she is new, her "skin" is more taut, the filling more robust. The backing fresh and clean. The new one is a lovely relief when she arrives in the mail, ordered by the breast prosthesis specialist at Nordstrom who has worked with me for six years now, who measures and fits and orders me just the right one. She even fills out the absurdly-thick stack of insurance forms for me.

No callback from Chip. Was this asshole ignoring me? Maybe he was out of town. I decided to call the rental agency and ask if someone can give me advice about how to reach someone (anyone!) who can run out to the house and fetch Water Boob from the drawer and send her home to me.

I was heading on another summer trip in a week, and really didn't want to have to deal with the hassle and expense of trying to get another prosthesis in time to be bathing-suit-ready. I didn't want to go boobless, either. Uni-boobs kind of suck the air out of the hot tub. The unspoken discomfort. The sympathy stares. The "I went through it too, sister" moments of profound connection, and the "I went through it too, you need to call my Pastor and come to church with me, he healed me, he can heal you, too" unwelcome intrusions.

As I worried about having to go boobless at the beach that next week, I thought back to the spa pampering day that my friend had treated me to, to celebrate finishing chemo. There was a bachelorette party happening at the spa that day. I did not have my wig on or my breast prosthesis in. I could tell that I was a buzzkill to the fresh-faced bride and her entourage. I could feel it in the awkward looks exchanged between the bride and bridesmaids as they saw my body in the sauna. I was the bald one with one breast. Just looking at me pierced the veil of youth and beauty that surrounded them. A part of me wanted to yell at them, "I was you not so long ago! I was a bride with two breasts, too! I had long hair, also! And YOU'RE the ones who are feeling uncomfortable right now?!"

The secretary who took my call asked how she could help. She had a sympathetic voice. I'm a sucker for a warm, maternal voice, and my walls came down. I told her that I left my prosthetic breast in a drawer in the hutch in the master bedroom at the house on Pochik, and that I just needed someone to go get it for me. I may have whimpered.

The secretary advised me to call Chip and leave him a more detailed message, so he understood the importance of this lost item.

"Hi, Chip. It's Laurie Pomeranz, John's daughter-in-law. Wanted to circle back and see if you can help me with that thing I forgot in the bedroom drawer at the house on Pochik. See, it's, ummm, my prosthetic breast. And I need it. It's in the little top drawer in the master bedroom. Could you please swing by the house send it back to me? That would be great. So sorry to trouble you!"

Within fifteen minutes, Chip called, "Laurie, oh my goodness! Heading there now!"

The next day, FedEx appeared, with my boob in an envelope. Not even a piece of paper to protect her, no note. Just a boob in an envelope. I had to laugh, thinking of Chip, in his Nantucket-red bermudas and boat shoes, opening that drawer and seeing my boob there, sunny-side up, looking right back at him, nipple gazing him in the eye. I imagine him using his fingers like pincers, touching it as little as humanly possible. Grossed out and fascinated, wary of cooties, glad to get this over with, and dropping Water Boob into a FedEx envelope.

I imagined the series of delivery people who shepherded my left breast home, where she now sits in the skinny top drawer of our dresser, right beneath the photos of days gone by, days before my breast was lost, and could be returned by mail.

CONTRIBUTOR PROFILES

Allison B.
At age forty, Allison went in for her first mammogram and came out with a cancer diagnosis. After three major surgeries, she is thrilled to be 100% cancer-free. She holds deep gratitude for her precious young daughter and caring, beloved husband who lovingly held her hands through every moment of this difficult journey. Allison is the head of user experience design at a tech startup and is a former Vice President of Design at a Fortune 50 company. She loves 1940s-style swing dancing, creating raw food delicacies, and capturing unique photographs of life's special moments.

Merijane Block
Merijane Block writes personal essays, creative non-fiction, and occasional poetry, with a focus on living with life-threatening disease and compromised physical function. She has lived with breast cancer for twenty-five years, twenty of them Stage IV, and has presented at conferences, patient advocacy forums, medical schools, and on public radio and television. From 2004-2008, she had the honor of facilitating the BAYS support group for young women with breast cancer. She is particularly passionate about contributing to the continuing education of clinicians, and changing the medical narrative to one consistent with the actual experience of individual patients. Her work appears in *Art.Rage.Us., Art and Writing by Women with Breast Cancer, The First Look* by Amelia Davis, *Lake: A Collection of Voices, Volumes Five* and *Six*, and online at *Birdland Journal, Work by Laguna Writers.*

Jen Brand
Jen was diagnosed with invasive breast cancer at age thirty-five, when her girls were just fourteen months and four years old. She has fought hard through a bilateral mastectomy, chemo, hysterectomy and adjusting to surgical menopause at thirty-six. Thanks to the support of BAYS and the nonprofit First Descents,

Jen is stronger, healthier and happier than ever before. She lives in Berkeley with her husband of thirteen years, her daughters Talia (twelve) and Minerva (eight), and her seven-year-old puggle, Ozzie.

Natalie Buster
Natalie is a recruiter in San Francisco. In her free time, she practices yoga therapy and can be seen singing and dancing on various Bay Area stages. Originally from Wisconsin, Natalie spent a good portion of her life in New York City as an actress/singer. Natalie lives in Walnut Creek with her husband Conrad.

Meaghan Calcari Campbell
Meaghan has roots in small-town Illinois and now calls San Francisco home. She works in philanthropy and ocean conservation with local communities and non-profits. Diagnosed with breast cancer at thirty-two without a family history of the disease, her initial treatments lasted sixteen months and will now continue for many years. Meaghan finds great joy in serving as President of BAYS. Her essays were published in the *The Day My Nipple Fell Off* and *Shivering in a Paper Gown.* She has traveled to fourteen countries and paddled three rivers since her diagnosis in 2012, and looks forward to more adventures with her husband Mike and dear friends. To see more of Meaghan's writing, visit http://keepingabreast.me/.

Kara Carter
Kara was born on the East Coast and made London her home for nearly twenty years. With her British husband Dene in tow, Kara moved back the United States in 2013 to turn her professional passion for transforming health care systems to her native country, on the eve of implementation of the *Affordable Care Act.* As it happened, she got to experience the system from the patient perspective, when she was diagnosed with breast cancer just nine months after arriving in San Francisco. Kara now lives in sunny Oakland with Dene and their rescue dog Ronin. She loves vegan food, board games, British comedy, Japanese animation, long walks during the day and quiet nights in.

Deborah Cohan

Deborah is a mother, dancer, physician and rabble-rouser
spreading messages of joy, interconnectedness and love. As UCSF
Professor of Obstetrics/Gynecology and Zuckerberg San Francisco
General, Deborah runs HIVE (www.HIVEonline.org), a hub of
reproductive and sexual wellness for those with HIV. At forty-
four, Deborah was diagnosed with breast cancer—she danced the
day of diagnosis and nearly every day throughout treatment,
including in the operating room. A friend posted a video of the OR
flash mob which instigated a pop-up social movement of joy and
healing through dance. During chemo, Deborah hosted a
Meditation Mob, a Gratitude Mob, a Composting Mob and a
Listening Mob. Through her Foundation for Embodied Medicine
(www.embodiedmedicine.org), Deborah offers teachings in
embodied presence and dance for medical providers and those
facing health challenges. When not mothering, dancing or
delivering babies, Deborah likes to meditate and explore primary
sensory experiences in nature.

Kelsey Crowe

Kelsey lives in San Francisco with her husband, daughter and
pets. She is a Board member of BAYS, and authored a book with
Emily McDowell called, *There Is No Good Card For This: What
to do when life is scary, awful, and unfair to the people you love.*
She hates this disease and loves the women she has met by
having it.

Sarah Haberfeld de Haaff

Sarah never fancied herself a writer, but fell into it by way of her
breast cancer experience. She worked with young children as a
speech pathologist in San Francisco. Diagnosed initially in
August 2011, she tackled chemotherapy, a bilateral mastectomy,
and radiation, all while potty-training one child, Gabe, and
preparing the other, Sophia, for kindergarten. Sarah was
diagnosed with metastatic disease in August 2013. She readily
admitted that she could live life so fully because of her husband
Greg and family and friends in their amazing circle around her.
Throughout her surreal journey, she carried herself with dignity,

humor, openness, warmth, bravado and determination. She taught us all what it means to live with integrity, even through suffering. Sarah died from metastatic breast cancer on February 23, 2015 at the age of forty.

Ami Dodson

Ami is a recovering lawyer who spent twelve years working in various legal communications jobs. She now devotes her time to advocating for and helping young women recently diagnosed with breast cancer, which she believes is better for pretty much everyone. She lives in Lafayette, California with her husband Scott, her son Asher, and her daughter Avah—to each of whom her contributed story is dedicated with love. And to the memory of all the Ricks and Joes in this world who enrich our lives beyond what they can possibly imagine.

Wendy Donner

Wendy is an educational consultant and writer living in Marin. She is currently working on an educational research project focused on maker-centered learning. Wendy found writing her blog, We GOT This, to be an invaluable tool during her cancer treatment and her pieces have been featured on the *Huffington Post* and *Momastery*. In her free time, she can be found riding her bike up the Marin hills and romping around with her husband, two children, and rescue poodle, Star. To see more of her writing, visit www.wendydonner.com.

Alexandra Fraser

Alexandra Fraser is an environmental scientist who is passionate about urbanism. She leads the environmental approvals for major civil infrastructure projects that serve and transform our community. Trained as a plant ecologist, Alexandra's PhD research modeled biodiversity patterns in the Swiss Alps and Greater Yellowstone Ecosystem. During graduate school, she met her architect husband through the bicycle scene in a Midwestern college town. Alexandra rode a bicycle century the weekend before she learned she had breast cancer. Her diagnosis at age thirty-four came shortly after her third wedding anniversary. Alexandra and her husband never knew they wanted to have children until a doctor told them that cancer treatment would leave them infertile. Another doctor offered a then-experimental fertility preservation technique. Today, they are raising their son in downtown San Francisco's colorful Tenderloin neighborhood.

Erika Gee

Erika is an educator, administrator, and cultural worker. She has worked in various museums and nonprofits in San Francisco Bay Area, Los Angeles, and New York City. Armed with new insurance upon her return to the Bay Area, she was diagnosed with breast cancer. She wonders if the other provider did a crappy job with first mammogram just a year before, or, cancer grows damn fast. She is grateful for her fierce co-workers, all her doctor friends, and her aunt and uncle for their support and care during treatment. Erika is currently is a community planner working in San Francisco's Chinatown.

Chelsey Hauge

Chelsey is a media artist and writer, and is currently a Postdoctoral Scholar at Brock University. She holds a PhD in Education from the University of British Columbia, and her research interests include digital literacy, youth media production, and girl-led activism. Chelsey was diagnosed with breast cancer in 2013, and found great healing in the arts. Never before a songwriter, Chelsey nervously agreed when her incredible friend Kate Reid proposed the idea of writing a song together, shortly after Chelsey's mastectomy. Kate has a Master of Arts in Social Justice, and a Bachelor of Education from the University of British Columbia, and she delivers keynotes, concerts, and workshops for secondary and post-secondary schools and professional organizations (for more information about Kate, please visit www.katereid.net). After the song was written and recorded, Chelsey proceeded to listen to it approximately four thousand times. You can find out more about Chelsey at www.chelseyhauge.com.

Naked Heart
Naked Heart never fancied herself as a poet, but poetry started pouring out of her after her breast cancer experience. After cancer treatments, she and her survivor friend realized while hugging each other that they could literally feel each other's hearts. This led to the choice of pen name. Naked Heart lives in San Francisco and is an aspiring writer. In her free time, she hikes the Marin headlands exploring new trails. She also loves to meditate, ride her bike, dance, swim and climb the Coit Tower steps during lunchtime.

Rebecca J. Hogue
Rebecca is a part-time professor and PhD student. She was diagnosed with bilateral breast cancer only three weeks after moving to California from Canada. She blogs about her experiences in all its absurdity and emotions at http://bcbecky.com.

Kate Holcombe
Kate feels lucky every day for her loving husband and their four wonderful children. She feels doubly lucky to do meaningful work she cares about deeply: empowering individuals in their own health, healing, and personal development through Yoga, regardless of background, experience, or financial means. As Founder and Director of Healing Yoga Foundation (HYF), a nonprofit project of Commonweal, she has been supporting those facing cancer and other life-threatening illnesses and challenges for over twenty years. Her twenty-five-year study of yoga philosophy proved to be invaluable throughout her cancer adventure. See www.healingyoga.org/articles to read many of her published articles on the Yoga Sutra. She strongly encourages women to do regular self-exams, having found her own lump within weeks of "clear" mammograms that missed it. She is eternally grateful for the wealth of resources, loving support and her incredible community of friends who all showed up for the ride.

Cat Huegler
This is Cat's second contribution to a BAYS anthology, this time trying to be funny and wondering if her "friends" will remember their comments. Cat's been dealing with this cancer life since being

diagnosed a week before her wedding in 2013. Currently in the middle of hormone treatment, she continues to make her husband, friends and family exhausted with the constant quest for fun—yet not allowing fun to get in the way of naps. Between fun, Cat works in tech, managing meetings and conference calls around hot flashes. Cat would like to give a special shout-out to her super strong support system from Reading, Pennsylvania to Oakland, California and everywhere in-between, even New Jersey. You fools keep it moving forward.

Erin Williams Hyman
Erin was an editor of arts publications, the mother of two amazing boys, wife of a loving and intellectually-matched Rabbi, and a fierce Scrabble competitor. Her previous life as a Lit professor made her passionate about storytelling in all its forms. She believed that speaking the truth about our lives is essential to healing. More of her writing can be found at bmatzav.blogspot.com. Erin was the curator and editor of the first BAYS book, *The Day My Nipple Fell Off.* Erin was and is a model of strength, elegance and grace. With great magnanimity, purpose and fierce intellectual inquisitiveness, she lived and loved fully. Erin died from metastatic breast cancer on September 18, 2014 at the age of forty-two.

Emily Kaplan
Emily just passed year three since her second diagnosis of breast cancer. You may have seen Emily featured in the Scar Project, a series of large-scale portraits of young breast-cancer survivors. Visit the Project at www.thescarproject.org. Having turned her passion for wine into a career, she enjoys traveling to experience the wine and food culture of other countries. She lives in Berkeley with her husband and two kids, Samara (ten) and Micah (eight).

Ann Kim
As the daughter of a doctor, Ann grew up thinking that she would follow in her father's footsteps. When she realized that she could not stand the sight of blood, however, Ann pursued a career in law. As a founding Board member and past President of BAYS, Ann

feels grateful to fulfill her childhood dream of helping people through illness, just in a different way than she had originally planned.

Mary Ladd
Mary Ladd's writing has appeared in *Playboy, Ozy, San Francisco Weekly*, and KQED. She is the author of *The Wig Report*, a book project packed with comedic riffs on oozing infectious sores, constipation, hospital hotties and illness. Mary endured twenty-two rounds of chemo, seven surgeries, eight infections, forty-nine blood tests, and completely lost her hair, eyebrows, and thirty pounds. She is a San Francisco native and member of the San Francisco Writers' Grotto and has eaten (calf) brains on TV with Anthony Bourdain. http://www.wigreport.com/

Sara Mahdavi
Sara is a Bay Area native who has traveled the world but only moved as far as Los Angeles, for law school, before returning to San Francisco. When she found her breast lump, Sara and her family were on a two-and-a-half-month adventure to Turkey, where Sara was interviewing Syrian and Iraqi refugees for resettlement in the United States, and their son was becoming accustomed to being treated as a little sultan of Istanbul. Sara thought the lump surely could not be cancer because she was only thirty-eight, active, and healthy. Sara has remained active through her chemotherapy and radiation treatments and faces ten years of hormone therapy after that. When she was diagnosed, Sara was just at the age—by San Francisco standards, at least—to be having a second child, which is what caused her to draw the parallels she did for her story in the book.

Julie Morgan
Julie started her life on the east coast and travelled west until settling in San Francisco in 2003. She has spent two decades in hospitals working as nurse. Julie began volunteering with the advocacy nonprofit Breast Cancer Action shortly after her breast cancer diagnosis at age thirty-seven, and served on the Board of Directors for several years. She used to spend most of her time in

the mountains or on the dance floor, but is now seen more often at the playground with her toddler, Danika.

J. Mork

J. is a longtime resident of San Francisco. She has written and performed in the San Francisco Bay Area focusing around issues of disability and sexuality. J. loves to travel and has an ability to make any hotel an erotic wonderland or a writing retreat. The travails of navigating between continuing after-effects of breast cancer treatments and living in the today is J.'s everyday project.

Laura Pexton

Laura loves adventures and laughter with friends and family. She has had a fulfilling career in the medical field as a nurse practitioner with a doctorate degree in nursing. She has traveled to over forty countries and has participated in eleven humanitarian medical missions to far flung places. She was diagnosed with breast cancer in 2001 at age twenty-eight, just after her daughter was born. She has been in treatment for metastatic breast cancer since 2004. Her message to others is to live life beyond limits! One person CAN make a difference.

Laurie Hessen Pomeranz

Laurie is a San Francisco–based marriage, family and child therapist, who works with teen-aged boys and their parents. She is a proud mom of a teen-aged boy, and a grateful partner in an eighteen-year marriage. Laurie is a singer and dancer with a local tot-rock band, and she moonlights as a Director with Beautycounter, coaching a team of Consultants and educating people about safe skincare and cosmetics. She is in her happy place when she is watching her son, or the San Francisco Giants, play baseball. Laurie's writing has appeared in *Salon.com*, and in the anthologies *The Day My Nipple Fell Off*, *Shivering in a Paper Gown*, and *I Am With You*.

Angela Raffin

Angela is a Midwesterner at heart, despite living in the Bay Area for twenty-eight years. With a penchant for smiling at strangers in public, she is told at least once a day, "I feel like I know you from somewhere? You look just like…" Her tweenage daughters find this especially endearing and not at all embarrassing. Angela is a clinical social worker at a Regional Center, serving individuals with developmental disabilities, working to see more opportunities for these folks to integrate into our workplaces and communities. Diagnosed at forty-three with Stage IIIA breast cancer on a Tuesday afternoon, the months since have been manageable primarily due to a super husband, family, friends and BAYS.

Yamini Kesavan Ranchod

Yamini was raised in Michigan, and transplanted to the Bay Area in 2011. She is an epidemiologist by training, and was diagnosed with Stage II breast cancer at age thirty-one, after finding a lump herself. When diagnosed, she was half way to completing her PhD at the University of Michigan, studying social determinants of health. After a year of initial treatments including chemo, radiation and Herceptin, she moved to Berkeley, California. After completing her PhD, Yamini joined UC-Berkeley as a post-doctoral fellow to continue her research. Against the odds, Yamini conceived a baby girl three years post-treatment, and she is currently tackling mothering a one-year old while navigating the trials of continuing preventive treatments. Yamini enjoys swing and salsa dancing, cooking, traveling, the outdoors, and spending time with loved ones. She is incredibly grateful for the support of her family, friends, and colleagues over the past six years.

Janet S.

Janet fancies herself an athlete; she snowboards, rock climbs, practices yoga, and hikes. She also loves music and dancing. She was diagnosed with breast cancer at age thirty-two, metastatic at thirty-four. At age forty, she had her third recurrence in her liver. Despite ongoing treatment, she is thriving—still climbing mountains, backpacking and traveling the world.

Sia Sellu

Sia is a San Francisco native who was first diagnosed in 2012 while in exile in Portland, OR. Sia is an award-winning community activist. She is very active in social justice issues. Housing, child care, police brutality and education equity are some of the causes she has worked tirelessly for over the years. She also advocated for Whole Foods to return its Kale Yeah! Juice to its shelves without wheatgrass. She is most proud of her daughter Arianna, who she raised as a single mama. Arianna is an educator and revolutionary. Sia continues her walk with cancer, as the disease has progressed as of April 2016. She plans to laugh, fight for her causes and make out with really hot dudes for the rest of her life.

Andrea Ghoorah Sieminski

Andrea currently writes about her crazy adventures with a new baby, post-cancer, on her blog *A Girlfriend's guide to life after cancer and infertility* at comfortablynumb.co. Her writing has also been featured on the *Huffington Post*. Sieminski lives in San Francisco's Mission District with her husband, daughter and dog. Her entire family, including the dog, are avid Buffalo Bills fans. She earned her JD from Duke University School of Law. Prior to becoming a stay at home mom, Sieminski practiced corporate law for two national law firms, as well as a Bay Area start-up company. She was diagnosed with Stage I triple negative breast cancer in October 2012, and concluded her treatment in July 2013. Happily, she continues to be NED (no evidence of disease).

Jill Sakol Snow

Jill is a devoted wife and mother of two energetic young boys who loves adventure travel and living in San Francisco. She has an MBA degree from New York University and works as a senior credit analyst at a large mutual fund investment firm. She met her future husband in 1996 on a ski trip in Vermont. After finishing graduate school that year, the two of them traveled together in Africa for three months where they realized that they were falling in love. They have been married for seventeen years and have had many adventures together including backpacking through the Costa Rican rainforest, traveling across the Continental United

States, and most recently taking their boys on the trip of a lifetime to Ecuador to canoe along Amazonian rivers and explore the Galápagos Islands by boat. Jill was diagnosed with early stage breast cancer at age thirty-nine, and had a recurrence of metastatic, Stage IV disease four years later. While this diagnosis and cancer treatment have had a profound impact, she maintains her hopeful attitude by keeping active with her family and spending treasured time with friends. She recently climbed Mount Shasta with the Breast Cancer Fund to raise awareness of the environmental causes of this disease.

Marla Stein
Marla, her younger sister, mother and maternal grandmother are all breast cancer survivors who do not carry any known genetic mutations. Because she listened to her gut and advocated for herself, Marla found her lump at an early stage. Due to her age, she underwent chemotherapy and a bilateral mastectomy. As an advocate, Marla has previously served on Breast Cancer Action's Board of Directors and worked for the Breast Cancer Fund. Marla also mentors a teen girl through a local non-profit and enjoys volunteering. For fun, she spends quality time with her friends, takes her dog to the beach and always has her passport ready to go! Originally from New York, Marla is thrilled to call San Francisco home.

Lindsay Jean Thomson
Lindsay is a champion for finding the best in yourself and others. She's a teacher, writer, and the co-founder of Women Catalysts, a community dedicated to helping women get ahead without losing their hearts. Lindsay lives in San Francisco with her dog Leo, who she found walking down the highway in Anderson Valley one beautiful spring day. Anything is possible!

Trinh Vuong
Trinh moved with her family to Modesto, California from Vietnam in 1979 at the age of three. She currently runs a small salon in Pleasanton and has been a cosmetologist for twenty years. She was living in the South Bay when she was diagnosed with breast cancer

in 2011. She then moved back to Modesto to be closer to family. In 2013, she had a local reoccurrence of breast cancer. Since her original diagnosis, she has traveled to many destinations and is knocking off bucket list items along the way. She loves spending time with her family, friends, her boyfriend and two dogs. Being surrounded by the people she loves has been the greatest support system for her recovery.

Lori Wallace

Lori, a San Jose, California native, was diagnosed with early stage breast cancer a week before her youngest son's fifth birthday. She believed that treatment would take her out of commission for a few months, maybe a year, and then she would be "back in the game," trying to save the world, while raising her two boys, and loving her crazy family. That did not work out. Treatment was crippling and recovery was slow. Soon after returning to work, she found a new lump. Her cancer had progressed to Stage IV, metastatic disease, with no cure and median survival being two to three years. Lori is now forty-five years old, with an awesome twenty-five-year-old son, Evan, and precious ten-year-old son, Braden. She has redirected her passion for sustainability and local community to breast cancer activism and is living life condensed, squeezing as much fun as possible, between rounds of chemo, while loving family, friends and life even harder.

Robin Bruns Worona

A professional copywriter, Robin spends all day, every day playing with words. She recently relocated to Portland, Oregon with her husband and four-year-old twins after nearly two decades in San Francisco. While she misses the rolling fog and majestic city skyline, she is thoroughly enjoying the greenery and laid back attitude of her new home town. You can find more of her musings on twins, cancer and exploring a new city at fishmilksalad.com.

Kristen Zeitzer

Kristen loves living in Marin with her incredibly lovable son, Xander. They dance, hike, and play when not at work or school. She tackled several surgeries, chemotherapy, and radiation after her Stage III breast cancer diagnosis in June 2014. To celebrate one year later, she rented a hot-air balloon and learned aerial-yoga. After two years, she rode dirt bikes in the Colorado Rockies and hiked Joshua Tree. She is presently planning other adventures with Xander and her besties.

Doreenda Ziba
Doreenda enjoys jumping waves on the beach, kayaking, and biking. In the past year, she has moved cities, got a new job, a new apartment, and has made lots of new friends. But, she misses her BAYS ladies something fierce. To see more of her writing visit sitforabit.mindpress.com.

"Things falling apart is a kind of testing and also a kind of healing. We think that the point is to pass the test or to overcome the problem, but the truth is that things don't really get solved. They come together and they fall apart. Then they come together again and fall apart again. It's just like that. The healing comes from letting there be room for all of this to happen: room for grief, for relief, for misery, for joy."

— Pema Chodron, *When Things Falls Apart: Heart Advice for Difficult Times*

ACKNOWLEDGMENTS

The editors would like again to honor and remember our beloved sister, Erin Williams Hyman, who first recognized the stories that the Bay Area Young Survivors women have to tell the world. She continues to inspire us to put words onto the page.

We wish to express our deep gratitude to the authors, who courageously and unabashedly put their experiences on paper.

We are grateful for the wisdom offered by the following storytellers, doctors, writers, poets, love warriors, philosophers, and teachers: Margaret Atwood, Paul Kalanithi, Joan Didion, David Whyte, Cheryl Strayed, John Green, Jack London, Glennon Doyle Melton, Mark Twain, Haruki Murakami, and Pema Chodron

Lastly, we acknowledge all of the women of the Bay Area Young Survivors—those who have gone before us, like Erin, Sarah, and so many, too many, more, and those who stand beside us. As Ram Dass said, "We're all just walking each other home."